QUAKERS
and the
ENSLAVED
in
NORTH CAROLINA

QUAKERS *and the* ENSLAVED *in* NORTH CAROLINA

J. TIMOTHY ALLEN

Published by The History Press
An imprint of Arcadia Publishing
Charleston, SC
www.historypress.com

First published 2026

Manufactured in the United States

ISBN 9781467159005

Library of Congress Control Number: 2025944973

We are very clear in our judgment, that Friends having kept such numbers of slaves, did much contribute to the ruin of their posterity: for the poor negroes were put to do nearly all the work, while the children of Friends were brought up in "pride, fullness of bread, and abundance of idleness." (Eze.XVI:49), riding about for pleasure, living at ease and in fullness: this was productive of many evils, and opened wide doors for unprofitable and pernicious intimacies with hurtful company, until, alas, the poor youth in some particular places are almost all departed from the way of truth, and almost total desolation reigns in some places in this land…Oh! the mischief of idleness and oppression.

—Quaker Job Scott (1775), in Hinshaw, Carolina Quaker Experience, *130*

North Carolina Yearly Meeting occupies rather a unique position among the American Yearly Meetings. Situated as it is in a section of the country in which slavery was for so long a paramount issue, and lying as it does too far south to be much influenced by the modern currents of population, there has resulted from these two causes a sort of provincialism among North Carolina Friends, which characterizes them wherever they go and which has made their history in many respects unlike that of any other yearly meeting on the continent.

—Julia S. White, "History of North Carolina Yearly Meeting," 2

North Carolina's majority slave-holding lawmakers blunted every effort of Quakers to free their slaves from 1777 until the 1820s.

—Tise and Crow, New Voyages to Carolina, *94*

CONTENTS

ACKNOWLEDGEMENTS

A historian utilizes many sources. Some are found in libraries and online; others are actual people. I would like to thank the following for their wisdom, advice and knowledge: Ron Osborne of Spring Friends Meeting; Kay Davis Coltrane of Centre Meeting; Dee Lewis, The History Museum of Carteret County; Wendy Cummings, the North Carolina History Center at Tryon Palace; Noah Janis and Lori Meads, the Museum of the Albemarle; the staff at Newbold-White House; Brenda Haworth of Springfield Friends Meeting and director, Museum of Southern Domestic Life; Joshua Brown, pastor of Springfield Friends Meeting; eminent Quaker historian Max Carter, Guilford College; Gwen Gosney-Erickson, Guilford College Quaker Archives; Dr. David Cecelski, North Carolina historian; Lisa Cox, interpreter at Alamance Battleground State Historic Site; James Shields, the African American Cultural Arts and Historical Center in Burlington; Sarah Carrier (thanks for your patience!), Wilson Library, University of North Carolina–Chapel Hill; Alison Thurman and Domonique Romero, North Carolina Department of Natural and Cultural Resources; Laurie Smith, Alamance Historical Museum; and Steve Miller, good friend and fellow co-writer.

INTRODUCTION

The need for a book on Quakers and slavery in North Carolina can be summed up by dissecting the information on a historical marker in the town of Halifax: "Escape! The Roanoke River, Halifax, and the Maritime Underground Railroad." The town of Halifax, settled along the Roanoke River, was a major port in 1700s North Carolina, a crossroads of trade routes and commerce from far and near. "Taverns, print shops, and docks served as valuable sources of information that could be crucial to the success or failure of a runaway." After noting that fugitive slaves relied on a network of information available from other slaves and free Blacks who also used the intricate routes of the rivers and waterways for their escapes, the sign informs us that "a community of antislavery Quakers lived across the river from Halifax. An 1830 newspaper article reported that they removed more than 600 persons of color from North Carolina." The marker was erected by the National Underground Railroad Network to Freedom. The tourism intent of the sign is obvious: Come to Halifax, where there was a station on the Underground Railroad run by North Carolina Quakers.[1]

From the tourism side of history, this historical marker is a well-intended and much-needed effort to discover and advertise Underground Railroad sites in the Tarheel State and across the nation. It continues the well-known association of Quakers as antislavery conductors on the invisible tracks of the Underground Railroad (URR). It correctly describes the little known but major component of the URR now referred to as the Maritime

Underground Railroad (MRR). More importantly, it emphasizes and elevates the overall role of Blacks, slave and free, and correctly diminishes the role of whites in the plight and flight of fugitive slaves. It implies that one small community of Quakers (identified as Rich Square Meeting in the above noted teaching plans) was responsible for helping six hundred Blacks to freedom (the teaching plans say three hundred). And it cites an 1830 newspaper article as proof.

Conclusion? This certainly *has* to be a Quaker URR site!

On further investigation, the sign is yet another instance of what I am beginning to call "the equation." Local lore + some facts + speculation X and an assumption or two = another story about Quakers, runaway slaves, and the URR. The marker implies that Quakers did not own slaves, perpetuates the myth that all Quakers were against slavery, and suggests that all Quakers were involved in what is called the Underground/Maritime Railroad.

As we will see, there is more to the story.

The "article" was simply a brief *notice* that Quakers in general in North Carolina, not just in Halifax, had placed over six hundred "people of color" into new and free lands and that four hundred more awaited their turn for freedom. These numbers equate nearly exactly to the number of slaves deeded to the North Carolina Yearly Meeting by Quakers and some non-Quakers. They were called "Free Negroes." Rich Square Meeting, however, was not just "across" the river; it was twenty miles away from Halifax. The minutes of Rich Square Meeting reveal they were *against* secretly moving slaves to freedom, as in the URR. Rich Square's brief published history mentions no involvement in anything like an URR.[2]

In reality, fugitives headed toward Halifax relied on the wits, wisdom, and information of local Blacks, free and enslaved, as well as some whites, a few of whom were Quakers, possibly from Rich Square Meeting, on a perilous route either to reunite with family in the area or journey toward freedom on the Maritime Railroad.

STEPHEN WEEKS, IN HIS 1896 work *Southern Quakers and Slavery*, states, "Slavery was *the* subject which differentiated Friends in the South from other religious bodies." He further asserts, "The mission of Quakerism has been to the slave....They announced their opposition to the system when it had other opponents, and they steadfastly maintained their testimony until its last traces were swept from the English-speaking world." In a 1958 reminiscence, Olive Rogerson Stallings, who lived in the Perquimans area, states bluntly that "Friends were not allowed to own slaves." This is curious, because in her article she mentions Thomas Newby, who, we will learn, was the first Quaker of conscience in North Carolina who wanted to release his slaves. Thus, it should come as no surprise that many, including Quakers, believe that the Society of Friends has always been against enslavement.[3]

Weeks's and Stallings's overall assessments are typical, but when investigated further, the road to that steadfast testimony was anything but linear and smooth. Jean Soderlund concludes, "The century-long struggle over slavery within [the Religious Society of Friends] was essentially a journey over unmarked ground." Weeks and many other Quaker writers in the past do not address fully the issue of Quakers who *enslaved* other humans. Closer to North Carolina, Quaker Algie Newlin properly acknowledges that the Society of Friends, in their first hundred years, "failed to make a strong stand against slavery," further noting that Quakers "who had become scattered from Barbados to New England" had acquired slaves. Still, he never explores this darker side of Quakers and enslavement.[4]

In 1940, some fifty years after Weeks's history was published, Herbert Aptheker asserted, "There is a prevailing general impression that the Quakers represented, as a body, throughout their history a solid phalanx aligned against human enslavement." He goes on to conclude, however, that the tediously slow process of full opposition to slavery by Quakers nationwide indeed did not come to fruition until just before the Civil War. Quakers Donna McDaniel and Vanessa Julye describe the confusing reluctance of past Quakers to fully and forcefully undertake the arduous journey to full emancipation of the enslaved and the total abolition of enslavement.[5]

This work explores that tedious and slow process, that "journey over unmarked ground."

In North Carolina, the journey was a long, arduous, roughly 150-year trek, and it included many detours and dead ends. Surprisingly, most Quakers, while against enslavement, were indifferent and even averse to the matter of manumission or abolition. Some were *gradualists*: as they worked out the numerous complicated legal, social, religious, and even economic obstacles involved in the manumission process, they would gradually reach abolition. Some were *segregationists*: they wanted freedom for Blacks but not inclusion within the Quaker Society. And last, some were *paternalistic*. They wanted Blacks freed, yet they wanted to control them socially and religiously by leading them up in the way of white Quakers rather than letting them live life the way they desired.[6]

Thus, there are two sides of enslavement. Quaker slaveowners were enslaved by the life and culture of enslavement as well. For many Quakers, as for many whites in general in the colonies and early America, north and south, ownership of slaves was a symbol of social status. Quakers, however, slowly realized that their life of wealth led to sloth, and thus they fell away from the sober tenets of Quakerism such as thrift, industry, and a simple lifestyle. And for Quakers, this might have been the real reason for their push for manumission and the abolition of slavery. The sin of enslavement was leading the Quakers astray and threatening the very soul of their faith.

NEARLY ALL NORTH CAROLINA Quakers either hailed from the North or had long genealogical roots to the North, and enslavement, sadly, was part of these roots. Rhode Island and Massachusetts were "seeded" by white enslavers from Barbados. Booker T. Washington states bluntly, "No one section of our country was wholly responsible for its introduction, and, besides, it was protected for years by the General Government." Solomon Northup's enslaved ancestors were from Rhode Island. New Englanders were involved in the capture, use of, and trade of slaves before it became the "peculiar institution" of the South. Slaves in New York were treated just as harshly as they were in the South, and the lower Northern states were not the safe havens for free Blacks that we have been led to believe. Thus, there was a reason for the irony that "New York City became both a site from which fugitives fled bondage and a destination for runaways." Harriet Jacobs (writing as Linda Brent), a formerly enslaved woman from

This is the only known portrait of Harriet Jacobs, dated from 1894. She hid for seven years in a tiny attic crawl space in a house in Edenton from 1835 to 1842. *Public domain, Wikimedia Commons.*

Edenton, North Carolina, affirmed this assertion. Slavery was an *American* problem, not a Southern aberration. And American, not just Southern, Quakers were part of this problem.[7]

Anthony Benezet instructing colored children. Historical poetical and pictorial American scenes, by J.W. Barber, 1850. *Public domain, Wikimedia Commons.*

New England Quakers in Boston and especially Newport bought and even traded in slaves. Newport was the center of the transatlantic slave trade, contributing over 60 percent of the total American slave trade. In 1762, Quaker Anthony Benezet called out the "Inhabitants of *Pennsylvania*" for their part in the enslavement trade (his emphasis). Indeed, Quakers up and down the Atlantic coast were entangled within the web of enslavement. Tarheel Quakers, nearly all of whom had genealogical, economic, and social ties to the North, trudged through nearly ten decades of debate and introspection, leaving behind the cultural acceptance of, and economic dependence on, enslavement, moving to a stance of gradual manumission and finally arriving at full emancipation. While it may be tempting to criticize the snail-like pace of this journey and its immediate problems, the result of what Quaker historian Seth Hinshaw calls a "sublime indifference to consequences," we will find that their compassion and tentative actions often delayed emancipation *to the benefit* of the enslaved, a story in itself that is too neglected or, given today's sensitivities, condemned all too quickly.[8]

English Quakers and, eventually, Quaker settlers in colonial America profited from enslavement. Quakers were industrious to a fault, and this industry included the sale and transport of the enslaved. Indeed, around 1756 the Pemberton brothers in Pennsylvania were prime examples of a conflicted Quakerism as it tackled slavery among its own ranks. The brothers sought to end enslavement among Quakers, but they continued to trade in humans as long as others outside the Quaker fold needed enslaved workers. For them, slaves were a commodity—like fruit, cattle, and lumber—to be traded. Even as late as 1854, slaver ships with possible Quaker connections were captured in New York. Ironically, John Woolman, the Quaker most responsible for first standing against slavery, planned a trip on a Pemberton ship to the West Indies to preach against enslavement. Even Quaker abolitionists such as Thomas Garrett were suspected of profiting from abetting fugitives.[9]

Another economic reason for the slow development of antislavery within the Quaker ranks was that many Quakers depended on the labor of their enslaved. As farms grew, as shops expanded, as shipping found new opportunities, and, importantly, as the supply of available white indentured workers diminished, new labor was needed to fill the ranks. Along with this, "The slaveholders had invested sizable sums to buy their bondsmen and bondswomen....They had taken the time to train them in specific jobs, and felt they needed their labor." To immediately emancipate their slaves meant huge losses for their businesses, shops, and farms, which would have to close until other workers could be found. This would also affect the greater economy of cities.[10]

Third, there is the Quaker tenet of waiting until all are convinced, all are *clear*, by the Light to move forward to settle a problem. (In my research for my book *North Carolina Quakers: Spring Friends Meeting*, I found it took Spring Meeting years to decide on whether to fix a leaking roof.) Ironically, there were often mitigating circumstances where it was wiser and more humane *not* to manumit the enslaved. Typically, there was a period of about twenty years between a fervid call for a change in one aspect of Quaker slavery and an actual adequate response. Unexpected complications often arose. For example, when Quakers freed their enslaved, many formerly enslaved were recaptured and sold back into servitude. Dealing with this legal conundrum led to Quakers retaining their enslaved until a more feasible answer could be found. Thus, it became evident that a solution often took debate, reflection, and reevaluation coupled with a compassion that would, to us, and no doubt, to the enslaved, exhibit an initial hardness of heart and even indifference before matters were resolved. On top of this, the North Carolina General Assembly, led by slaveowners, fought these efforts with law after law that required more time to evaluate and thwart.

There was one other important issue to address: What to do with enslavement when the Bible clearly supports it? Quakers waited for further clarification. Seth Hinshaw illustrates this tedious and often frustrating pace with the intriguing tenet of a Guiding Light: "The Quaker belief in continuing revelation enabled them to see that the practice of slavery in Bible times did not prevent the coming of further light." He further shows that the "Quaker conscience gradually became sensitive, *aware*" (his emphasis). He then cites North Carolina Quaker Nereus Mendenhall:

> *This guiding is not completed this day or next, this year or next, this century or next, but goes on* progressively, *by and through the Spirit, as it has guided, is now guiding and will guide the individual and the human race.*[11]

This was especially true in Quaker deliberations concerning enslavement. While it may seem to us cut-and-dried, black and white (literally), emancipation, as often noted by many of the Founding Fathers of America, was not an easy decision. Within the debate, serious questions arose. Was it really fair to free the enslaved when it could, and did, lead to recapture and then even worse re-enslavement? Was it really fair to release slaves with no skills whatsoever, no land, no tools, no education, and expect them to be successful and thus not have to be a burden on the populace? Recalling his experiences in Philadelphia and the benevolence of the Quakers there, former slave (of a Quaker merchant!) Olaudah Equiano suggested that, for some enslaved who worked for good masters, it would be best to remain in bondage than to risk recapture, which, sadly, happened with the very first slaves released by North Carolina Quakers. Still, along that bumpy, often muddy, Quaker road of measured wisdom and emotional rhetoric, the enslaved embarked to their new life of freedom as Quaker slaveowners also ended their dependence on their enslaved, which greatly affected their comfortable lifestyles.[12]

As Quaker abolitionists arose within the ranks of staid and seemingly apathetic Friends, they were driven by three tenets of the Quaker faith. First, all people were equal in God's sight; thus, they believed that the Light of God resided within each person. This did not mean, however, that Blacks were seen as intellectual, social, and economic equals. Second, Quakers were nonviolent, and stealing a person by force to enslave them was deemed a violent act. Helping a fugitive run away was tantamount to stealing and thus violent as well. Third, enslavement induced a lavish, lazy lifestyle that conflicted with the Quaker beliefs against ostentation and sloth.[13]

NORTH CAROLINA QUAKERS, BOTH coastal and Piedmont, were connected to the outside world. Many once called home New England, Pennsylvania, Maryland, Virginia, South Carolina, England, Barbados, and other Caribbean Islands. Through these connections, Quakers shared meeting minutes and queries with one another, even correspondence overseas from the London Yearly Meeting. North Carolina Quakers left relatives and friends "back home," yet they stayed in touch and shared the events, news, and publications of their time and place. Quakers also consistently traveled short and long distances to visit other meetings. Coastal Quakers in North Carolina were connected by trade to all parts of the world, from commercial ports in Rhode Island, New Jersey, New York, and Pennsylvania to the Caribbean Islands, east to Africa, and portions of Europe. North Carolina Quakers were not isolated from the world; indeed they brought their worlds with them as they settled the wilderness of Carolina. And part of that world included the acceptance of enslavement.[14]

Quakers arrived in North Carolina in the 1650s, and for about fifty years, they dominated the early governance of the colony of Carolina. North Carolina historian Milton Ready declares that "Quakers remained the most important group in colonial North Carolina until the American Revolution." This suggests that Quaker discussions concerning enslaved and enslavement, debates, and decisions, at home, in meetings, and in politics influenced colonial North Carolinians. Indeed, the first governor of North Carolina, James Archdale, was a Quaker. Quaker leaders lived on plantations and owned slaves. Quaker John Woolman, who visited many Quaker meetings and lodged with local colonial Quakers, was often "uneasy" about Quaker enslavers, but curiously, he was moved to explore his feelings in depth only after every visit to North Carolina. What was it about North Carolina Quaker slaveowners that moved him so? Woolman figured it out, and with his wisdom this practice would soon end, but in the meantime, on the benches, Quakers for and against enslavement worshipped together in silence, waiting for the Light.[15]

Theological discussions, many of which were quite heated, even theatrical, plagued the gradual movement of Quaker antislavery activism. As always, like other Christian denominations, Quakers began with the Bible, especially the teachings of Jesus. The Bible clearly condoned enslavement, as every Christian slaveholder and many non-slaveholders sympathetic to the peculiar institution reminded their antislavery neighbors. The Apostle Paul advised the slave Philemon to return to his master. Abolitionist Friends, however, produced other verses that offered another perspective. Jesus taught his disciples to render unto Caesar what is Caesar's and unto God what is God's (Mark 12:17). How does one "render unto Caesar" (obey the laws and statutes of the colony/state regarding enslavement) and "render unto God" (see all humans as equals, do unto others as you would have others do unto you, etc.) in the matter of enslavement? Many arguments and debates concerning abolition of enslavement centered on the teaching "Do unto others what you would have them do unto you" (Luke 6:31). How does one reconcile the enslavement of people with this teaching? The Bible, therefore, was not clear on enslavement. Quakers who silently sat in the pews on First Day meetings quibbled and argued the fine points of the Bible outside after the meeting as they struggled to find their answers within the Light.

Thus, the institution and culture of enslavement was much more complicated than we have been taught, and these complexities emerge when we explore the Quaker discussions that revealed contentious conundrums for the People of the Light. For example, Quakers often purchased a slave in order to give him/her freedom, but this benevolent and altruistic enslavement was illegal in North Carolina. This raised issues among the Quakers, since they felt that they should follow the law of the land. On the other hand, intriguingly, some Quakers staunchly opposed such a practice because, in their minds, the purchase of a human for any reason, even freedom, was considered participation in the institution of enslavement. Here we see yet again a curious and frustrating slice of Quaker thought and culture, a culture that could be deemed so narrow-minded as to perpetuate the very thing they were against. Indeed, many Piedmont Quakers left North Carolina because of the acute restrictions of Quaker discipline. Quakers could indeed be peculiar when confronting the peculiar institution.

Likewise, some North Carolina Quakers were bequeathed enslaved people in family wills or married a person with enslaved people. This was the case with Quakers John Newlin and Richard Mendenhall, who used them in their various enterprises such as mills or farms.

North Carolina former enslaved Harriet Jacobs relates a story that gives an answer from a slave's perspective. She was sold to a benevolent Friend in New York, thus finally freeing her from years of enslavement in a caustic Tarheel family. But as she related to her new owner, who now granted her freedom, "Being sold from one owner to another seemed too much like slavery." Did slaves purchased by Quakers with the intent of freeing them feel the same way in regard to their Quaker benefactors?[16]

As North Carolina Friends helped enslaved in their quest for freedom, some Quakers felt this act was stealing from another person or that it was aiding and abetting a crime and a criminal. Thus, following the Apostle Paul's admonition in Romans 13, they chose to obey the law and retain their enslaved while treating them well and providing them a basic education.

Tired of this timidity and, some conclude today, hypocritical mentality, some Quakers joined increasingly militant abolitionist societies and some even left their Quaker folds to join the more proactive, staunchly abolitionist Southern Wesleyans.

So, the exciting, sometimes clandestine, always intrepid, yet finally salvific saga of North Carolina Quakers and their resistance to enslavement and their involvement in the URR is much more complicated than it seems. The tensions within these neglected stories tell a greater tale. And they may provide some wisdom for us today as we encounter and confront other troubling practices in our own backyards and around the world.

The following account of slavery along the Quaker Road unfolds into many somewhat overlapping episodes. First, Quakers, like many others in their day, enslaved others. Second, eventually leaders among the Quakers began to see the contradiction between their acceptance of enslavement and the New Testament teachings where Jesus envisions a different, egalitarian view of society. A few—emphasis on the word *few*—strong voices emerged within the Society of Friends, sometimes vociferously, other times gently, if slowly, nudging reluctant Friends to rethink servitude altogether and release their bondsmen and women. Third, roadblocks to Quaker manumission—cultural, theological, legal, and economic—had to be confronted creatively, and this led to much conflict within the Quaker fold. Once the Quaker consciousness was pricked, the Society of Friends realized it was not so easy to manumit their enslaved. Colonial laws and then state and federal laws tested their conscience and patience. Fourth, creative methods were contrived to emancipate and then move enslaved to safe territory, some of which, oddly, involved the very purchase of slaves. Fifth, after colonization to Africa failed and as more Northern cities and states barred enslaved and freed Blacks from a new life of freedom, all that was left was the clandestine URR and MRR that whisked runaways, freed Blacks, and even Confederate deserters, pro-Union Southerners, and escaped Union prisoners from the South to the North, to the west to Tennessee, east to the North Carolina and Virginia coast, and farther north to Canada.

I HAVE TRIED TO address these issues in the following pages using maps, meeting minutes, journals, letters, newspapers, podcasts, and interviews as well as current research from today's scholars previously unavailable to past writers on this subject. This includes oral history, which, admittedly, many scholars are loath to cite. But I found what I will call oral history 2.0—that is, the numerous family histories, personal blogs, and websites and local county histories as well as local lore connected with state historic sites. Ever since the publication of *Like a Family*, the excellent exploration of Southern mill towns that relied on oral histories, I think the use of some oral recollections of Quakers and slavery is appropriate. Thus, my reliance on "oral" histories.

In the final chapters on the various clandestine railroads to freedom, I focus more on the *interaction* of Quakers and enslaved and freed Blacks rather than a detailed investigation of the Underground Railroad itself. I hope to publish a full account of the URR in North Carolina in the future. Until then, you can read *Slave Escapes and the Underground Railroad in North Carolina*.[17]

The index for this work includes mostly people and place-names.

Nomenclature shifts as scholars move within and even create new social, cultural and academic approaches, understandings, and sensitivities in our histories. Thus, *slavery* and *slave* are now *enslavement* and *enslaved*. When a cited author generally employs the term *slave*, I have retained this description when referencing their information. To help the general reader make this transition I have interchanged these terms throughout the following pages.

Much thanks is given to the folks at The History Press for all their help in this project.

Finally, a thank-you goes to my wife, Jackie, who, some years ago, stated what most people incorrectly believe: "I thought all Quakers were against slavery." Thus began this journey.

There is more, much more, to this story but editorial constraints necessitated only the larger picture. Our journey down this Quaker road reminds us that, as with any contentious issue, the road to a solution is fraught with detours, dead ends, and angst. But the destination, the resolution, *freedom*, both for the enslaved and those enslaved by the culture, society, and politics of the peculiar institution, is worth every step on the way.

QUAKERS AND ENSLAVED IN EARLY COLONIAL CAROLINA

At first the slaves were treated very humanely, often as one of the family, and were fed and clothed as the son or daughter.
—Addison Coffin, "Early Settlement of Friends," 39

In 1765, Friend John Griffith voiced some of the worries of attentive Quakers of conscience in the early to mid-1700s. Evidence from the past suggests that "slavery formed an important source of wealth, prestige, and power almost everywhere in the province" of North Carolina. Equally important, Black enslaved filled a labor void that was hindering production and thus economic mobility among the ever-industrious Quakers. As the enslaved became the norm in servitude in the early to mid-1700s, new laws emerged to ensure their compliance to the expectations and prejudices of North Carolina whites, especially wealthy slaveowners. The enslaved fought this process by remaining true to their African traditions, culture, and religion. Thus, a vicious circle emerged. Resistance by bondsmen and women brought about even stricter laws, which made those enslaved more resolved to withdraw to their own culture. And this stubbornness, often described as savagery, led to more punishments and legislation. Quakers were caught in the middle.[18]

Enslaved servants and Quakers both entered the colony of North Carolina at about the same time in the mid-1600s. While Virginia and South Carolina were *slave societies* featuring a planter elite and huge plantations, North Carolina was more a *slave culture*, since only four planter families are recorded in early North Carolina. This distinction between slave society and culture lies in the fact that early North Carolina never had a staple crop like tobacco or cotton, no large port, and only a small number of towns along with a weak government.[19]

In 1723, John Brickell embarked from Ireland to the colony of North Carolina, where he lived for two years in Edenton. Back in England, he wrote the first history of North Carolina, which was published in 1737 when the colony was about seventy-five years old. His observations about life in the eastern portion of the state provide a firsthand context for our exploration of Quakers and enslavement.

Brickell recalls the trickle of settlers "in *Albemarl* [*sic*] County by several persons from Virginia, and other Northern Colonies." The land was abundant and cheap, and the soil was so fertile that these settlers became "Numerous and Rich." Once word spread of the success of these few settlers, the region lured families from the "Neighbouring Colonies" and "several Parts of Europe" for "pleasure and profit; which makes the Planters in a great measure live after a most luxurious manner." The only thing lacking in this land of plenty was "a sufficient Number of Hands, and Industry, to make it as fine a Country as any in the World." Industrious Quakers were among those settlers, and their industry soon led to the need for more laborers.[20]

It was this lack of sufficient hands that forced settlers to consider other means of what was then called "industry." In the past, men, women, and even children would indenture themselves to a master of a family for a time, generally three to seven years, sometimes longer. This "sale" was to cover the costs of their passage from England to the colony, but one could also sell oneself to cover excessive debts incurred in England or in the colony. During this time of indenture, they were considered servants who were basically part of the family. In this time, many were apprenticed to learn a skill. Since many indentured servants were convicts or social deviants (the British often alluded to the colonies as populated by thugs and vermin), part of the indenture experience was learning basic social skills as well as some education, especially religious education. Quakers were encouraged to follow this "civilizing" regimen.

Brickell's observations delineate what is expected of both masters and servants. Scholars assert that at this time in the settlement of northeastern

North Carolina, "in practice, indentured servitude differed very little from outright slavery." Those in bondage were considered property, could be punished severely, and even worked to death. At the completion of an indenture, the owner was to provide "each Man Servant a new suit of Cloathes, a Gun, Powder, Shot, and Ball, and ten Bushels of *Indian* Corn," and "fifty Acres of Land." This amount of land could not sustain a small farm, so it was often sold by the freed servant. While these gifts were indeed generous, Brickell laments that they would not support an independent farmer. The best gift, however, was the skills the servant acquired while indentured. The freed servant could then be employed by the former owner or referred to another plantation owner for work, where he received one-seventh of what he produced for his new boss. In reference to badly behaved servants, Brickell observes that they "are rather greater slaves when made free" because of a poor work ethic and lack of skills. These observations emerged when Quakers discussed manumission. In short, servants and slaves, once released, were to be fully prepared to live on their own without becoming a detriment to both themselves and their community.[21]

Brickell related conditions around 1730 when he describes the treatment of enslaved men, women, and children. First, enslaved Blacks in North Carolina were either from Guinea or born on a plantation. Those from Guinea were difficult and bellicose while those "bred and born" ("stud" slave men were encouraged to have more than one wife to produce more children) on the plantation were "more industrious and honest and better Slaves than those brought from *Guinea*." Brickell believed that this is "particularly owing to their Education amongst the *Christians*, which very much polishes and refines them from their barbarous and stubborn Natures." He continued with yet another method to induce proper behavior: terror. Harsh penalties were required to deter slaves from harming their masters, stealing, or fomenting insurrections. Given this observation, we have to wonder if Brickell's comments here are, overall, in reference specifically to Anglican enslavers who were known to be quite cruel to their slaves. It was this cruel treatment that Quakers were admonished to avoid.[22]

Brickell's observations focus on eastern coastal North Carolina, where plantations with high enslaved populations were more the norm. The Lower Cape Fear region, where few Quakers settled, held the highest concentration of enslaved and the largest slave plantations. Conditions were different in the western portion of the state. Those who enslaved were only about 10 percent of the population in the Piedmont areas in the mid-1700s. On the North Carolina–Virginia border, where tobacco was the cash crop, 40 to 60 percent of families owned slaves. Writing in 1899, a generation after slavery ended in North Carolina, John Spencer Bassett provides a bucolic, even romantic, yet otherwise accurate description of Piedmont North Carolina slavery:

> *Here the farms were small. The slave-owners had but few slaves. With these they mingled freely. They worked with them in the fields, ploughing side by side. The slave cabins were in the same yard with the master's humble home. Slave children and, indeed, slave families, were directly under the eye of the master and, better still, of the mistress. On such farms five to twenty slaves was a usual quota, although their number often went to fifty and even higher.*[23]

Some Blacks born in North Carolina, according to Brickell, could read and write, and some were taught trades, while others simply learned the pedestrian ways and means of the plantations.[24]

While the aforementioned expectations were the ideal, sadly, most enslaved were typically ill-fed—about a peck of meal per week, maybe some meat, and whatever vegetables they could grow in their small gardens, assuming they had time to garden at all. They were ill-clothed—generally given a suit of clothes and two shirts and one pair of shoes for the new year. As the year went by, the clothes became more threadbare and the shoes worn out. Children and some adults wore little to nothing. Slave quarters were minimal. Many slave cabins featured dirt floors, maybe a loft, one cot, or a straw mattress. Gaps between the logs or slats were chinked with mud to keep out the cold and rain. The slave was given one blanket a year, sometimes one every few years. These conditions varied depending on the benevolence of the owner.[25]

All of these issues would be addressed by the Quakers as they struggled both to free themselves from the yoke of enslavement and free their enslaved from bondage.

BY THE MID-1660S, SETTLERS from Virginia had already trickled into the northern part of what was then the Carolina Colony. Most, if not all, were poor, disaffected servants and squatters who claimed whatever piece of land suited them. Others were still running from poverty and their criminal ways in England. All were considered runaways, rogues, bandits, renegades, and villains and were compared to the filth at the bottom of privies.[26]

Afterward came more "respectable" settlers who could afford Creoles, slaves who were born in or lived for some time in the West Indies or the Caribbean and were thus used to living with whites and understood their language and their customs and culture. Many were of mixed European African descent and, while still enslaved, lived somewhat amicably with their white owners.[27]

The first slaveholders and enslaved arrived in North Carolina from Virginia in the late 1600s. Milton Ready points out that "masters in North Carolina, most with fewer than five slaves, worked alongside their helpers in the laborious tasks of clearing trees, draining swamps, tilling the land, and planting crops." Along with this, unlike South Carolina, "blacks sometimes gained an unusual degree of freedom overlaid with only a thin façade of their own African culture." As the Cape Fear region was settled after 1729, small numbers of enslaved peoples in ships laden with other cargo arrived in the colony from Bermuda, New York, Jamaica, and, mostly, from Charleston. In the early to mid-1700s, the enslaved population shifted from Creoles to Africans. These enslaved "overwhelmingly worked as field hands and artisans on farms and plantations and as domestics in white homes" while a small number worked in towns or in the maritime industry. This culture did not foster the retention of old individual African traditions and rituals but instead grew into a heterogenous amalgam of disparate African customs. Still, despite the efforts of various missionaries and itinerant ministers, including Quakers, most enslaved retained their unique African religion. While some Quakers tried to include their enslaved in their normally staid religious meetings, their efforts were generally met with indifference.[28]

When the Carolina Colony split into North and South Carolina in 1713, new laws specific to the northern region were legislated, and these included tighter restrictions on both the enslaved and servants. Further restrictions, now much harsher, were enacted in 1741 with another revision of slave codes, much of these concerning the increase in runaways and focusing more on the enslaved than servants. The period between 1715 and 1741 brought about a major shift from white indentured servitude—the culture that Virginians brought with them to the Albemarle region in the 1660s—to an increasing enslavement culture emerging on the larger plantations in the Cape Fear area. It also created and fostered a social boundary between white servants and Black slaves, a distinction that previously was not discernible.[29]

This distinction, as well as others, was of major importance in the discussions among Quakers concerning their enslaved. One point highly relevant for Quakers applied to North Carolina servants in the 1715 act. Masters were required to teach their servants reading and writing; furnish food, clothing, and shelter; and not punish them excessively. At the end of their indenture, servants were to be given new clothes, some tools, and a small tract of land. And this was the accepted norm regarding slaves as well in the Quaker household.[30]

Since many Friends were from William Penn's colony, Quaker Pennsylvania provides a model for understanding the attitudes of North Carolina Friends concerning their servants and enslaved. White servants were treated no differently than Black servants in Pennsylvania in the 1680s and vice versa. Indeed, as Jean Soderlund points out, "Differences in the legal status of white and black bondsmen were unclear," and the assumed racial inferiority of Blacks would not fully emerge until the 1730s. Thus, "most Friends probably had about the same attitudes on slavery as other colonists." Likewise, it was expected that Black "servants" would be released after some years of service just like white servants. There essentially was no difference in a slave and a servant in the late 1600s in the colonies except that the enslaved were held in servitude longer than servants. Within a generation, however, racist attitudes about the differences between whites and Blacks emerged among Quakers who described them as "slaves" rather than "servants" and held them for life rather than manumitting them.[31]

Kay and Cary point out that "African languages, institutions, values, and worldviews exerted a powerful hold on slaves and the cultures they shaped." Thus, "it would not have been easy for owners to convert such slaves to ruling class values." As Quakers in the Tarheel colony followed their traditions and tried to teach slaves skills, languages, religion, and social niceties, their attempts were often met with indifference. These barriers and the resultant assumption of Black ignorance and thus inferiority no doubt led to some, perhaps many, Quaker enslavers assuming racist views, breaking away from Friends values, and mistreating their enslaved out of sheer frustration.[32]

After the Carolina Colony was divided into North and South in 1713, and as the enslaved population increased while the servant population dwindled, the genesis of a major shift occurred. The diminishing pool of white servants from which to find labor for farms and industry led to an increase in slave imports, most of which were from the African nation of Guinea. African captives were more apt toward bellicose behaviors of resistance, especially running away. This led to new legislation in 1715 addressing the growing issues regarding enslavement, especially runaways, and enslavers and society in general. Along with this legislation, the distinctions between white servants and Black slaves fully emerged, and enslaved people were now regarded as degenerate and savage. By the 1750s, North Carolina was fully a slave culture, white servitude a thing of the past. And within this culture, slave codes became harsher. It was also at this time that Quakers sympathetic to the plight of the enslaved found themselves in conflict with many of these laws.

According to Ready, Quaker influence on the early years of the Carolina Colony was profound and most obvious in the northeastern corner of the colony. When the Carolina Colony was divided into North and South, fifty years of Quaker influence, dominance, and religious compassion over the northern region ended. We have to wonder if the increase in punitive laws and the growing divide between servants and slaves in newly formed North Carolina was at least in part due to the loss of the more lenient and humane influence of the society and politics of the Quakers. The slave code was amended in 1741 and again in 1753, 1758, and 1764, and each revision included harsher penalties and restrictions on slaves and those who aided and abetted runaways.[33]

A review of the progression of these codes reveals the growing oppression of enslaved peoples and the increasing legalization of enslaved as chattel.

The Act of 1715 defined the "social, economic, and even physical place of the Negro population." Bondswomen and men traveling without a ticket were to be apprehended by all whites. Fugitives absent more than two months could be killed with impunity. The enslaved who performed "honest & Faithful service" could be freed, but runaways could not. Emancipated slaves had to leave the colony within six months or would be sold back into enslavement. Along with this, those harboring a runaway more than one night were fined ten shillings per night. The fine increased to two pounds in 1741 for those who encouraged the enslaved or servants to leave their masters. Last, the enslaved could not congregate in any way for any reason, including worship. On the other hand, masters were required to teach their servants a trade and to read and write and furnish them with clothes, food, and housing. At this point in North Carolina, there was a clear distinction between slaves and servants. Still, severe punishments were restricted by law.[34]

In 1723, all Blacks, free or bond, above the age of twelve were considered taxables. In 1729, a statute was enacted to prevent the enslaved from traveling at night, and if a slave hid for over two months, he/she was to be shot. Overall, religious instruction was not encouraged and the enslaved still could not congregate.

By 1741, labor in North Carolina had almost completely transitioned from servants to slaves. New laws focused on runaways, slave insurrections that might stem from runaways, and manumissions that might lead freed slaves to revolt against their former masters. For example, runaways who failed to surrender could now be killed or destroyed with impunity.[35]

Punishments for the enslaved included hangings and public whippings, but only runaway enslaved heads might be cut off and displayed on pikes. This horrendous practice eventually subsided, only to be replaced by a more "humane" branding, burning, scarring, and amputation of body parts. Ironically, fearful enslaved people fled Virginia for North Carolina, most heading for the Great Dismal Swamp and coastal towns such as Wilmington, Edenton, and New Bern. Thus North Carolina had a reputation as a haven for runaways—white, Black, servant, or slave—which resulted in stricter legislation. Some whites aided runaways in these coastal areas, and many, if not most, were Quakers.[36]

According to Kay and Cary, "Running away represented perhaps the most significant of slave crimes." The act was an embarrassment for enslavers, whose very reputation centered on their ability to hold their bondspeople in check. Whites also feared runaways would gather and start insurrections, as was the case in the Stono Rebellion near Charleston, South Carolina, in 1739. A similar rebellion nearly occurred in New Hanover County in 1767.[37]

Runaways were predominately young adult males, mostly field hands or watermen, most of whom were African, who had extensive knowledge of the lay of the land or rivers and sounds. Many of these fugitives ran off in small groups, but most fled individually. Slaves typically absconded during harvesting season, September–November, or February–April, the planting seasons. These were both times of hard work and good weather. Despite the lore of URR legends or the information concerning slave escapes during the holiday season, in North Carolina a minimal few fled during December–January. Slaves who had some command of English and a skill were the most successful.[38]

As a few daring Quakers slowly conceived plans to aid runaways and free their own enslaved, each of these laws placed them in danger. Fugitives often absconded at night, and Quakers gave them respite for days at a time. When the North Carolina Yearly Meeting began owning the enslaved to eventually give them freedom in the early 1800s or when a Quaker was deeded enslaved peoples as part of an inheritance so that they might be freed, the enslaved had to be kept until plans and funds could be collected for their move to the North. Such plans often took months to come to fruition. As the URR was "constructed," runaways often traversed the secret paths at night. On top of this, Quaker polity condemned breaking the law. Thus, it is no wonder that only a few intrepid Quakers dared break the colony's statutes or the Quakers' beliefs.

QUAKERS IN NORTHEASTERN NORTH CAROLINA

We had meetings also among the slaves, their masters appearing to encourage them to come; there were seasons of instruction both to slaves and such of their masters as attended.
—*Stephen Grellet,* Memoirs of the Life and Gospel Labors of Stephen Grellet, *147*

Halfway between Elizabeth City and Edenton stands the Newbold-White House, the first brick mansion built in North Carolina. The storied history of this story-and-a-half structure illustrates an important aspect of the complicated dynamic between North Carolina Quakers and enslavement.[39]

The land was originally purchased by a Tidewater, Virginia settler, Joseph Scott, in 1684. Scott left the Virginia colony for the better lands of the northern portion of the Carolina Colony and patented 640 acres on the Perquimans River in 1663 and the following year acquired 200 more acres. At this time, he had one servant, probably indentured, as he had several others with different names throughout his life. After a visit by Quaker founder George Fox in 1672, the family converted to Quakerism. Scott was involved in local politics and participated in discussions with rebels on the Culpeper's Rebellion in 1679. He soon was the owner of almost 1,000 acres, and the wooden dwellings of this plantation were substantial enough for political and court proceedings to be held there, all signs of wealth and notoriety. The lands were passed along through the years to various descendants and then purchased by an outsider. Eventually, Quaker Abraham Sanders, already a substantial landowner, purchased the land, on which he later built the brick house. Interestingly, the purchase may have included the eight enslaved of the previous owner.[40]

The Albemarle region was tobacco country populated by many impoverished residents. Quaker Abraham Sanders, who also hailed from Virginia, with the help of his wife, Judith, and six children and at least four slaves, produced a more diversified crop of corn, tobacco, wheat, indigo, flax, and rice; livestock; and barrels and shingles or shakes for roofing. In 1730, he built the historic, indeed, exceptional brick structure that still stands today. When Abraham Sanders died, he owned four slaves: Sambo, Beth, Old Blind Mingo, and Lame Mingo.[41]

Quakers were quite industrious, as seen in the varied crops and supplies produced on Sanders's land, and this industry brought much affluence, as seen in the probate records of Sanders, which listed over three hundred items. The one-and-a-half-story brick house, with its hall and parlor design, was considered quite extravagant for that time, an architectural reflection of the owner's affluence and a "blessing by God." Glazed bricks, a parapet,

Newbold-White House. *By the author.*

dormers, and leaded glass windows proclaimed the owner's wealth to the visitor. The house was much grander than the William Lane house or the frame house of Solomon Pool, "a Quaker of moderate wealth who seems to represent the typical middling Albemarle farmer of his day." Indeed, though a bit smaller than the typical house of a grand planter in Virginia, it loudly spoke of the owner's wealth and station in life. Such affluence built on the backs of slaves would soon be questioned by reformist Quakers.[42]

Land availability in lower Virginia decreased in the mid- to late 1600s. Freed indentured servants now occupied more lands; planters bought up more acreage; tobacco, the major crop of the area, had worn out the land; and the population in general was increasing, tripling from 1644 to 1662. While some migrated westward, the threat of Indians turned others southward to the untamed (by white European standards) and fertile soils of what could only be described as a wilderness, the "Albemarle frontier."[43]

Most of these hopeful settlers were poor famers, but some were "convinced" Virginia Quakers (people who were converted into the Quaker faith). While Virginia Friends fled south into the Perquimans region, others, such as the family of Henry Phillips (also spelled Phelps), sought respite from persecution in New England. This movement of Quakers, both Virginian and New England, was the first migration of Friends to North Carolina, and the first Quaker meeting was on Perquimans River in the home of Francis Toms.

Colonial Carolina, known for its toleration of all religions, was a stark contrast to the Anglican dominance of Virginia and the stifling religious climate of New England, where Puritan intolerance led to severe, even deadly consequences for Quakers. Henry Phillips left Salem, Massachusetts, and arrived in the Albemarle region in the 1660s. Based on an obscure note in William Edmundson's *Journal*, Phillips may have found a few more New England Friends in the Albemarle region when they moved there in 1665. George Fox preached at Henry Phillips's house in 1672. Quaker settlers were also joined by non-Quakers from Charleston and Barbados.[44]

The mention of George Fox and Barbados deserves a caveat. Fox, whose personal spiritual unrest led to the founding of the Society of Friends in about 1650, a period of tumult in England, visited Barbados in late 1671 into early 1672. There, along with fellow Quaker minister William Edmundson, he preached to island Quakers about the treatment of their enslaved peoples. Barbados was a sugar colony of England and was notorious for its cruel, barbaric treatment of the enslaved. Since "sugar production ate up slaves at a phenomenal rate," the life of a slave "did not last long on Barbados." Sugar was so profitable and the demand for it never-ending that the enslaved were worked to death to meet these production needs and then quickly replaced with no interruption in large profits. Were Quaker plantation owners part of this evil? Was George Fox addressing such abuses?[45]

A seventeenth-century painting of Geoge Fox, possibly by Peter Lely. *Public domain, Wikimedia Commons.*

Fox and other Quaker ministers held many meetings on the island sugar plantations, and some of the attendees would have been plantation owners who were not Quakers. Fox was falsely accused by local officials of encouraging the enslaved there to rebel. Fox taught his white and Black worshipers the basic theology of the Quakers. In his addresses to the "negroes" (he does not call them "slaves"), he admonished them "to be sober and to fear God, and to love their masters and mistresses, and to be faithful and diligent in their masters' service and business." Stressing the importance of the master to instruct the members of his family, Fox includes the "negroes and tawny Indians" within this plantation family. (Indians were often captured in the colonies and sold into enslavement on the islands.) The master was to instruct his family to pray "and to teach, instruct and admonish those in and belonging to our families." Concerning the "negroes" on the plantations, John Hull, who was traveling with Fox, noted that this family instruction was "also about training up their negroes in the fear of God, those bought with their money and such as were born in their families, so that all come to the knowledge of the Lord…and that their overseers might deal mildly and gently with them and not use cruelty as the manner of some is and hath been, and to make them free after thirty years' servitude." In short, Quakers should instruct their "negroes" in the ways of Quakers, treat their servants well, teach them to respect their masters, and release them within a respectable period.[46]

From Fox's recollections, these interactions and instructions seem quite benign. But when set against the realities of the day they seem naïve, insensitive, and perhaps intentionally tepid so as not to upset other Quakers. Journalist Howard French writes, "By the latter decades of the seventeenth century, in fact, sugar was becoming a central driver of economic activity in England." This century saw a shift from the early Portuguese dominance in slave sugar production to a rising dominance in a plantation slavery. This economic boon for England began in 1627 when it acquired the tiny, uninhabited island of Barbados. There, for the entrepreneurial investors in England, "sugar, big landholdings, and plentiful Black slave labor all came together for the first time." On plantations that often enslaved three hundred Africans, it did not take long for distinctions between owner and slave to emerge. By 1636, it had been decreed that slaves were in bondage for life.[47]

Surely Fox became aware of this during his visit there. Harsh Black Codes were enacted on the enslaved, who were generically deemed savage, uncivilized African brutes. Was Fox's demand that overseers treat their slaves better in response to the inhumane treatment of Blacks? High mortality rates were the norm—indeed, expected—and the average lifespan was less than seven years for the hapless enslaved. French concludes that "slave owners in the islands expected the burdens of labor, poor nutrition, and disease to bring the members of their Black workforce to an early death." The enslaved were held in such disdain that dogs ate the flesh of dead Blacks in the open. Slave shipments increased to replenish these seemingly planned deaths, and "by 1660, England had become the clear volume leader in the North Atlantic slave trade."[48]

Quakers were part of this economy in many ways. Some Quaker merchants settled on Barbados, and Quaker ships unloaded captured peoples and goods to the island. Quakers imprisoned in England were shipped there to populate the island, and many were in servitude as cheap laborers as well. By 1700, there were five Friends meetinghouses on the island. These Quakers trafficked in enslavement, sending their chattel to Philadelphia into the early 1700s despite calls to end the practice in the late 1600s.[49]

Thus, questions arise when considering George Fox's instructions to enslavers regarding their property. Mostly, was George Fox's apparent reticence concerning such abuses a polite way to avoid rocking the boat of an increasingly brutal system of enslavement among his own people? Did he see enslavement as a form of indentured servitude, as J. William Frost wonders? Frost goes on to suggest that "Fox assumed that converting both masters and slaves would end the immorality and abuses that he found in

Quakers in Barbados by Carolus (Carel) Allard, Orbis Habitabilis, Amsterdam, circa 1700. *Public domain, Wikimedia Commons.*

both parties." Or perhaps Quaker plantation owners were indeed treating their enslaved better than their island counterparts.[50]

In the next thirty years, many Quaker meetings were established in the Albemarle area, which at that time was divided into four regions: from east to west, Currituck, Pasquotank, Perquimans, and Chowan. The largest body of meetings was in the Perquimans precinct, with Perquimans Meeting organized as early as 1680. The next largest was in Pasquotank. Households or small gatherings of neighbors met in the following places: Upper Meeting House (Wells); Little River, established in 1700; Lower Meeting House (Old Neck); Symonds Creek; Narrows of the Pasquotank; Newbegun Creek; Piney Woods; and what is today the Newbold-White House. Smaller, unorganized meetings were held in homes.[51]

In the late 1600s, the economic rise of the British Atlantic World along with the emergence of the plantation system brought settlers to the northern Carolina Colony with visions of success and increased social standing. This "cultural drive" came from observing "the opulence of their compatriots across the Carolina and Virginia border" who grew cash crops such as tobacco, rice, and indigo. In North Carolina, however, the soil was not conducive to a cash crop economy. Thus, settlers sought to fulfill their dreams by diversifying their industry producing tobacco, rice, cotton, and naval stores as well as other crops such as wheat and starting businesses such as ferries and shipyards. Labor was about to diversify as well.[52]

In 1692, Quaker Agnes Fisher Trueblood, who lived near present-day Elizabeth City, enslaved one person, Diana. Agnes bequeathed Diana to her four children in that "one halfe of all the negro Children that shall be begotten or born of the body of my negro woman Diana" would be theirs. This practice separated the enslaved children from their mother and raises the question of who fathered these children. We have no answers, but it demonstrates that in many ways at this period, Quakers, like others, were finding ways to increase their enslaved labor pool with no further investment. A generation later, Amos Trueblood willed around twenty Blacks to his children and grandchildren. In 1698, at least two Quakers in the Albemarle region, Thomas Simons and Henry White, brought their enslaved to Quaker meetings. A generation later, Perquimans Monthly Meeting worried that Friends were working their enslaved on the Sabbath, a clear violation of the Ten Commandments.[53]

By the early 1700s, the availability of indentured white workers had diminished, and industrious Quakers soon enslaved others to fill the void and help their ventures prosper. Edward Mayo, a Quaker leader, enslaved 3 people. Councilman Francis Toms worked 1,150 acres with 8 enslaved along with various servants. Quaker merchant Patrick Henley owned 1,100 acres and 11 enslaved. Sea captain John Hunt farmed 1,300 acres and managed it with 6 Africans and 1 Indian. The Therrill brothers, William and Gideon, collectively owned 400 acres and 2 African and 4 Indian slaves. Timothy Clare's 3 enslaved Africans and 2 enslaved Indians worked alongside his 2 indentured workers. After the early 1700s, the number of enslaved in the Albemarle region increased as reliance on servants diminished quickly. Quakers continued to enslave others into the late 1700s, when Thomas Newby, along with other Friends—Caleb White, Joseph Henley, Sach (Zach?) Nixon, Benjamin Albertson, William Albertson, Chalkley Albertson, George Walton, and Thomas White—collectively planned to release their 134 chattels.[54]

Bondsman Job was eventually freed by his Quaker owner, Benjamin Albertson, and, along with his wife, lived on land that was given to him. While the close relationship between former slave and owner was to prevent harm to Job and his wife, he still was not "free." He and other freedmen and women were hunted by well-armed slave catchers and thugs assisted by vicious dogs. Sending his wife to Albertson, Job hid in the woods until he was discovered. Tied with a rope, he was marched to jail, never to be free again.[55]

At this same time, with the increased acquisition of enslaved people, the Quaker conscience was emerging as the system of enslavement came under scrutiny. Fred A. Olds, citing minutes from Symonds Meeting before 1709, finds that "very early in these records appears notice of the manumission of slaves and the expression of the strongest sentiments against 'human bondage.'" In 1738, Perquimans Monthly Meeting declared "that no frend [*sic*]...Shall Suffer yr [their] Negroes to labor on the first Day of the Week."[56]

This new anti-enslavement conscience was pricked even more after a visit in 1746 from New Jersey Quaker John Woolman, who felt "uneasy" with the Quakers' acquisition of "slaves," and his message took root at Piney Woods Meeting, the oldest continuous meeting in North Carolina. Its meetinghouse, along with the Wells Meeting House and perhaps others, was burned in 1758. Sources are mixed as to the cause. Locals are skeptical that it was burned by proslavery arsonists who were increasingly disturbed by the emerging Quaker anti-enslavement rhetoric and manumissions. At the same time, they feel that is a possibility. In this same period, Albemarle Friends lamented their neglect of the spiritual and intellectual edification of their enslaved. Friends at Simon's Creek moved to consider holding meetings for the enslaved, yet Old Neck Friends were not so moved. Perhaps inspired by the visit of John Woolman, Perquimans Monthly Meeting advised Albemarle Friends to hold meetings for their enslaved. All Quaker meetings in the region were then reminded to treat their bondsmen and women well. By 1759, the following meetings were holding worship services for enslaved people: Simon's Creek, Old Neck, Wells, Newbegun, and Piney Woods. By the mid-1760s, however, most of these meetings had ended.[57]

Inspired by John Woolman, Quakers, both eastern and Piedmont, began seriously questioning their approaches to enslavement in the mid-1760s, with New Garden Meeting in Guilford County calling for stricter measures than their eastern counterparts. In short, it was a battle between eastern Quakers, who enslaved more people and whose economy depended more on the institution of slavery, and western Quakers, whose lifestyle and culture were less dependent on bondspeople. By 1773, eastern Friends had decided they could not purchase humans except from other Quakers. It was a small but significant first step toward abolition for eastern Quakers. By 1776, North Carolina Friends had taken a stronger stance and declared that "slavery was unchristian and that it was the yearly meeting's duty to cleanse itself of members who violated this testimony."[58]

Simon's Creek Monthly Meeting is an example of this cleansing. In 1776, several members decided to sell their enslaved rather than release them, most likely to recoup the cost of purchasing them. The meeting tried to buy them back but was unsuccessful. In 1777, four men were disowned from the meeting for selling their enslaved. Other members released their bondspeople only for the sheriff to capture and sell them.[59]

Still, other Quakers remained obstinate. Wells-Perquimans Monthly Meeting disowned several enslaving members. Job Miller and Josiah Murdough were disowned in 1781, as was Isaac Barbour in 1784 for "selling negroes." In 1785, Foster Toms and J. Outland were disowned for hiring and selling "negroes." John Shepherd was disowned for selling "negroes" in 1787. Caleb Elliot and John Chappel were disowned for holding slaves in 1789. Jonathan Newby was disowned in 1793 for refusing to manumit his enslaved.[60]

In 1832, Quaker minister Raymond Green visited the Eastern Quarterly area of Quaker meetings. In his correspondence with his wife, he recalls his meeting at Simon's Creek in Pasquotank. Many enslaved were in attendance in the estimated crowd of two thousand. He then reports on his meeting at Rich Square Meeting. He summarized his tour in eastern North Carolina thus: "All the meetings in this quarter have been large and satisfactory. Much decorum and propriety of conduct have been observed in them, which I have thought the more remarkable as Slaveholders, Slaves, and free people of color, were in attendance, and sometimes largely."[61]

The story of Rich Square Meeting provides much fodder for our investigation of Quakers and slavery. Many of the Friends who settled in the Perquimans and Pasquotank region in the late 1600s eventually moved westward to Bertie and Northampton Counties, forming Rich Square Meeting in 1760. "Rich Square Monthly Meeting was settled just about the time when a few of North Carolina Friends were beginning to feel that slavery was evil from which the Lord was requiring the Quakers to cleanse their hands." From 1758 to around 1800, Rich Square Meeting deliberated how to remedy the enslavement issue within their ranks. One result of such deliberations was Richard Jordan, whose family moved to Northampton County and settled around Rich Square in 1768. Richard attended the North Carolina General Assembly several times in the 1790s on behalf of the enslaved.[62]

While Rich Square Meeting was "ever watchful that the needs of the 'people of color' were taken care of," it seems that "many of the members were slow to follow the advice and directives of both the Yearly Meeting and Quarterly Meeting." In 1793, Thomas Outland was disowned for failing to pay the enslaved he had manumitted. In 1814, John Lawrence was complained of because he sold two of his enslaved people (meaning he owned more who may have been considered free). In 1826, Patience Jacobs was complained of for keeping her enslaved from earning wages. And in 1862, Joseph Copeland was disowned for, among other sins, hiring a "slave."[63]

Still, following the advice of North Carolina Friends Yearly Meeting, Rich Square Meeting members participated in the complicated Quaker manumission efforts of transferring their enslaved over to trustees selected by the meeting. Catherine White of Rich Square Meeting released her bondspeople to the meeting before she headed back to New England. The meeting cared for them for twenty-seven years. By 1832, all had been relocated to free lands. Other members followed suit. Their enslaved were then cared for and hired out, and the wages from their labor were used to provide care and some income. In 1813, Rich Square Meeting gave an old enslaved woman named Hagar ten dollars to provide for her needs. The meeting even took in enslaved people who requested asylum from slavery, as in the case of Jesse Lawrence in 1838. The enslaved under the care of the meeting attended the weekly worship services as well. When the funds and situation were right, the enslaved now "owned" by the meeting were to be transported to free states or Liberia.[64]

One of the "prominent characters" of this meeting was John Peele, who was a "large landholder." Like other nearby Friends slaveowners, John Peele (or Peelle) enslaved sixty Blacks, and they were transferred to his sons Edmund and Thomas, who then transferred them over to the Yearly Meeting in 1809. Edmund's wife enslaved fourteen Blacks, and these were also transferred to the Yearly Meeting. Twenty of these "Quaker negroes" were sent to Indiana, while twenty-eight were sent to Liberia in 1827. There were fifty-eight others "who doubtless were also sent to Liberia." The aged and infirmed bondspeople, however, remained with their former master(s).[65]

There is another side of the Peele family, though, that, while embarrassing and damning, deserves mention. African American Andre Kearns traced his family back to the Peeles through DNA testing. His fifth great-grandmother Patsy White lived in Nansemond County, which is in Virginia just over the border from North Carolina. She was freed by her Quaker owners somewhere between 1782 and 1806.

The story is not so bright when he discusses his fourth great-grandmother Francis [Frances?] Peele. She was enslaved by Bertie County farmer Kader Biggs. In a practice that was quite common, she was "studded" out with a Black slave to produce more children. Former North Carolina enslaved man Jacob Manson recalled how some slaveowners had "certain strong, healthy slave men to serve the slave women. Generally they give one man four women." However, in this case, Kearns sadly notes, Francis was raped by Quaker Robert Peele, and she "produced" several children with him. Kearns does go on to state that Peele's grandson Edmund, a member of Rich Square Meeting, released 125 of his slaves and gave them $25 apiece for their voyage to Liberia.[66]

By the end of the eighteenth century, North Carolina Quakers deemed enslavement a "disownable" offense (banned from attending the business meeting). As we will come to see, the release of an enslaved person was complicated, and thus some Quakers were slow to manumit. The 1794 minutes of Jack Swamp Meeting reflect this transition. "None trade in slaves nor hold them as such and those that have them under their care Endeavors to use them well as their abilities will admit of." Here we see that Jack Swamp Meeting Friends who still "owned" seemingly freed Blacks employed them in some capacity while waiting for a proper time and method to free them entirely. Thus, for northeastern North Carolina Quakers, three choices emerged for those who enslaved: keep them but pay them wages, in essence free in all things except name; others sold their enslaved; and some ignored the official pleas of the North Carolina Yearly Meeting and continued enslavement with no remorse.[67]

Addison Coffin, in his *Reminiscences*, recalls that early North Carolina Quaker settlers treated their enslaved well. In 1800, Quaker minister Stephen Grellet, along with his friend John Hall, rode into Alexandria, Virginia, where they saw enslaved Blacks "wretchedly clad and fed" who were chained while working in the fields. A few days later in the "pine woods of North Carolina," they attended meetings with enslavers. Ministering around the area of Rich Square Meeting, where they lodged with Richard Jordan, and then in Contentnea Meeting, Grellet and Hall spoke about the "poor oppressed" Blacks and requested meetings with their enslaved. The enslavers "were fully persuaded we should not say anything to their slaves in their absence, that we would not say in their presence." Given permission to hold meetings with the enslaved, the services "which we had with these poor afflicted people" were "very satisfactory." While all enslaved were no doubt poor and afflicted, it is telling that Grellet, who consistently complained of the tortures of enslavement throughout his memoirs, did not mention anything like the chained persecutions of slaves that he saw in Virginia while among North Carolina Quakers.[68]

Nine years later, Grellet was back in the Perquimans and Pasquotank area. While at Newbegun Creek Meeting, he wrote, "We had meetings also among the slaves, their masters appearing to encourage them to come; there were seasons of instruction both to slaves and such of their masters as attended." Again, there was no mention of the depravity of the enslaved or of harsh treatment of them.[69]

Stephen Grellet, by William Miller. Date unknown. *Public domain, Wikimedia Commons.*

Several Quakers from northeastern North Carolina were concerned about the plight of enslaved people. George Walton married into the Newby clan and became a convinced Quaker. Led by a series of dreams beginning in 1772, he donned the mantle of antislavery and assumed a strong role among North Carolina Quakers as they struggled with enslavement in their ranks. He encouraged Thomas Newby, mentioned earlier, to manumit his enslaved Blacks. This would have been a difficult decision, as Newby was probably the wealthiest person in Perquimans, owning one thousand acres, a store, and shipping interests. Manumission would have devastating effects on his livelihood. Thomas Nicholson, born in Perquimans about 1715, served as a traveling minister in the Quaker faith. In 1767, he wrote "On Keeping Negroes," in which he argued for the gradual manumission of slaves. He then changed his mind, and around 1774–75 he penned the article "Liberty and Property" for the North Carolina Yearly Meeting, which argued for the immediate manumission of the enslaved. Interestingly, there is no evidence that the Yearly Meeting ever published the paper.[70]

Another eastern North Carolina Quaker who stood with the enslaved was Barnaby Nixon of Perquimans County. Born in 1752, "He advocated the manumission of slaves, and was engaged in the important struggle in their behalf in Perquimans and Pasquotank counties in 1777–78." He later moved to Virginia and continued his crusade for slave manumissions there.[71]

The story of the Winslow family in the Piney Woods area in Perquimans provides a generational dynamic to the enslavement problem in northeastern North Carolina. Caleb Winslow, "an antislavery Quaker" who may have helped runaways near the Great Dismal Swamp (according to J. Brent Morris), initially struggled to manumit his enslaved people in the late 1700s. In 1781, Perquimans Monthly Meeting organized a committee to meet with enslaving members to encourage them to manumit their chattel. As we will see, there were complicated legal, ethical, theological, and doctrinal issues to consider in the manumission of their slaves. Caleb Winslow, as well as at least twelve others, was visited by meeting members at least twice in the following years. According to family records, Caleb had "manumitted the people he enslaved." His son Nathan did not inherit any enslaved people, but he was known to be a major enslaver in the Perquimans and Chowan area. Nathan bought one Black person in order that she might remain near her husband, a practice some empathetic enslavers often followed. For this altruistic action, he was disowned by Piney Woods Meeting. He purchased other enslaved people, but it is not clear to what purpose. It seems he bought most with the intent to free them, sending some to Liberia and keeping others nearby. In the years before the Civil War, some well-intentioned Quakers pursued this same action. Oddly, many Quakers were caught in this ironic bind of purchasing the enslaved so that they might be "freed" in some sense. For many other Quakers, this practice was simply deemed another form of enslavement.[72]

QUAKERS IN CORE SOUND

It is too manifest to be denied, that the life of religion is almost lost where slaves are very numerous; and it is impossible it should be otherwise, the practice being as contrary to the spirit of christianity [sic] *as light is to darkness.*
—John Griffith (1765), in Weeks, Southern Quakers and Slavery, *203*

A trickle of Friends crossed the Pamlico River into the Albemarle Sound region around 1703, and by 1730 Friends inhabited the Cape Fear region above Wilmington. Soon Carver's Creek and Dunn's Creek Meetings were established (1740 and 1746, respectively). Thus, by mid-century, Friends held meetings in Hyde, Beaufort, Craven, Carteret, Jones, Bladen, and Lenoir Counties.[73]

Core Sound Meeting records inform us about Quakers and enslavement in this region. As word spread of the large pine forests along the North Carolina coast—meaning the potential of prosperous naval stores—New England and especially Rhode Island Quakers established new homes in the Core Sound area around 1720. With this influx of Quakers, Pasquotank Meeting eventually set up the Core Sound Meeting in either 1733 or 1736 (sources disagree). Core Sound Meeting received sixty pounds of financial support from Rhode Island Quakers to build their meetinghouse. Other Quaker meetings followed: Clubfoot Creek, Beaufort, Upper Trent (1791), Lower Trent (1791), Bath, and Mattamuskeet (1793).[74]

Core Sound Meeting members were wealthy merchants and farmers. Henry Stanton, who arrived in the Carteret area in 1721, is an example of the diversity of Quaker merchants. He owned a shipyard, brickworks, orchards, vineyards, and turpentine stills all on over three thousand acres, some purchased using the enslaved as currency. Upon his death, his enslaved were transferred to his son Benjamin. Robert Williams, who originally hailed from England and then moved to North Carolina by 1765, owned over one thousand acres, a saltworks factory, and the first brick house in the area, but keeping to Quaker simplicity, it was "plain." In January 1774, Williams took out an advertisement in *The North Carolina Gazette* concerning two "Negroes" who had escaped from jail, where they were so ill-fed that they were starving. Williams desired to find their owner rather than risk taking them back to jail where they would be starved or frozen to death. For such actions, he was known to some as a "benevolent man." He freed his "several hundred" enslaved in 1780 "when the Society of Friends manumitted theirs." This was a huge financial loss.[75]

William Borden Sr., a successful shipbuilder in Rhode Island, moved to the Newport area in 1732. Each winter, he shipped in laborers from Rhode Island to work for him. It is not clear if William Sr. was an enslaver, but his son, William Borden Jr., lost his enslaved in the American Revolution to the British in 1782. By 1790, Borden Jr. again enslaved forty-three Blacks, which made him the largest slaveowner in Carteret County at that time. Borden Jr.'s sons William and Joseph also enslaved Blacks, but in 1820, Joseph manumitted his—except for those belonging to his children. The Borden family eventually owned over twenty-one thousand acres. In an 1843 reminiscence, Quaker John Shoebridge Williams, whose family enslaved others when he was a child, called the area "slave country"—meaning there were more Blacks residing there than whites. His family clearly split over enslavement. Around 1800, part of the Williams's family, as did other Quakers in the area, migrated to the Northwest Territory, now known as Ohio and Indiana, leaving behind the enslavement culture their Quaker convictions could no longer tolerate.[76]

Borden Jr.'s extravagant house in Beaufort, still standing today, embodies a problem that existed in the Core Sound Meeting: leading meeting members were not adhering closely to the new spiritual discipline of frugality among Quakers throughout the colonies. Indeed, as Neva Jean Specht points out, "Friends from Core Sound seemed less concerned with upholding the Quaker discipline as strictly as their counterparts to the north in Pennsylvania and New Jersey." She alludes to the burgeoning reform movement among Quakers in Pennsylvania, especially where a return to simplicity required both the relinquishment of their enslaved, which brought them wealth and prestige, and restraint from public office, which likewise led to affluence and the lure of power. While Quakers

William Borden house, Beaufort, North Carolina. *By the author.*

removed themselves from public office in Pennsylvania, several from Core Sound, especially the Borden family, continued their political careers. Likewise, some were emerging as successful elite planters. The Borden family was the largest landowner in Carteret County, and they owned the second-largest contingent of enslaved in the county. In fact, William Jr. was given to a life of reproach, including excessive drinking, according to Core Sound minutes. As we will see, this is the very lifestyle that Quaker John Woolman believed to be ruining the Quaker values of simplicity and frugality. And all this opulence was built on the backs of their enslaved.[77]

In a curious and somewhat cryptic note from the Core Sound Meeting Minutes, it seems that the family of Joseph Dew worried in 1785 that they could no longer take care of their enslaved. This may have been due to economic disruptions, especially trade up and down the coast, that ensued after the Revolutionary War. This would then raise the question of what to do with them. Manumit and risk their re-enslavement? Treat them as free people in everything but name and perhaps hire them out to locals? The minutes did not answer these questions.[78]

Meetings came and went depending on migrations, deaths, and practicality. Core Sound Meeting diminished by migrations inland up to 1771 and then rebounded substantially as locals were suddenly "convinced" to become pacifist Quakers to avoid military service or provide economic support to the American Revolution. After the war, the meeting lost members due to post-Revolution hardships and strong antislavery beliefs. In 1812, members of Core Sound Meeting who refused to manumit their enslaved left the Friends to join their enslaving neighbors attending nearby Tuttle's Grove Methodist Church. Those remaining raised $300 and paid a wagoner to carry "a load of negroes" from Core Sound to Indiana. Sadly, Core Sound Meeting was laid down (closed) in 1841.[79]

What is quite clear is that Core Sound Meeting members nourished business ties to the Northeast. In the late 1700s, William Borden Sr. regularly brought Rhode Island workers to his ship works; Joseph Dew and Richard Williams often journeyed north on business. At this same time, Core Sound members began migrating northwest to Ohio and Indiana. These connections, northeast and northwest, would have been advantageous for the emerging Quaker Underground Railroad/Maritime Railroad. In 1795, the State of Virginia already worried about "shadows of a secret network formed to assist in the absconding of slaves" in nearby Hampton Roads. It is entirely possible that Quakers on the coast of North Carolina could have been part of this effort.[80]

TUCKED BETWEEN THE COASTAL Plain and the Piedmont of North Carolina is Wayne County and the area around Goldsboro. A lesser-known Quaker migration to this region receives almost no attention from the standard sources. This is unfortunate because, as we will see, there was an URR conductor operating out of Goldsboro.

Some Quakers left Core Sound Meeting to move westward into the Piedmont of North Carolina. This was no doubt because of the search for new and more fertile lands. A few families did not travel so far away from home. Beginning in the 1740s, Quakers such as the Cox family from the Core Sound Meeting as well as other meetings in Virginia soon moved to Wayne County around present-day Goldsboro. Soon there were several meetings, one in Quaker Neck in 1752 and another in Nahunta in 1748.[81] William Newsome, a member of Rich Square Meeting in Northampton County in 1770, moved south to Wayne County, where the 1790 census lists him owning one enslaved. His son Joseph also enslaved one Black person.[82]

QUAKERS IN PIEDMONT NORTH CAROLINA

Deep River, my home is over Jordan…
Deep River, Lord, I want to cross over into campground.
—Black spiritual, date unknown

The Piedmont of North Carolina has long been associated with the Quakers. The area encompasses the present-day counties of Wilkes, Iredell, Surry, Yadkin, Davie, Stokes, Forsyth, Davidson, Guilford, Randolph, Montgomery, Alamance, Chatham, Moore, and Orange and is often described as the Quaker Belt by many historians. Scots-Irish, Germans, and Quakers, each with a history of persecution, settled throughout the region, and their reputation as dissenters made the Piedmont a hotbed of contention when the Civil War erupted. Many residents stood against slavery and secession.[83]

Running through much of this area is the Deep River. While not significantly deep, it slices a lazy southwesterly path through rocky banks that are steep, rough, and slippery. Many runaways fleeing to New Garden Meeting in Guilford County in hopes of freedom had to cross the Deep River at some point. The spiritual "Deep River" originated in this region, perhaps where the Quaker Deep River Meeting stood.[84]

The "replanting of Southern Quakerism" was a slow but progressive movement of Quakers from Pennsylvania and Nantucket as well as New Jersey and Maryland before 1725.[85] Settling briefly in Maryland, they then pushed into Virginia, but wanderlust guided them even farther south. A few hardy and adventurous Quakers from New England and coastal Carolina settled on the rich soil of the North Carolina Piedmont region beginning in the late 1740s. In the 1750s, this trickle of individuals and small families soon turned into a stream of immigrants.

Their reasons were many. Growing disagreements between successful and more worldly Quakers and the more traditional, simple Quakers were escalating, especially in Pennsylvania. There was also the lure of a new life on the frontier, escaping growing escalations with Indians and a reversion from the affluent, political lifestyles of Pennsylvanian Quakers who refused to give up slavery to a more pensive, inward, and quiet form of life and worship. For North Carolina Quakers, it most likely included fleeing the slave culture of the North Carolina coast in general. Yet the one common factor for all was economic: the lure of cheap, fertile land. Ironically, working this land would require slave labor if Quakers were to compete economically with their non-Quaker neighbors.[86]

The first Quaker meeting in the Piedmont was Cane Creek Friends Meeting, in what is today the small area of Snow Camp, North Carolina, about twenty-five miles west of Chapel Hill. Quakers, mostly from Pennsylvania and Maryland, settled along Cane Creek around 1749. Settlers in the area typically bought small land grants from two hundred to six hundred acres. In 1751, Cane Creek Meeting was established by Little River Meeting in Perquimans County, some two hundred miles eastward from Cane Creek.

Cane Creek Friends Meeting birthed numerous Quaker meetings, many of which were on a route that an 1808 map labeled "Quaker Road." Cane Creek Meeting ministered to and influenced Quakers from present-day Greensboro to Hillsborough. As more Quakers settled in the Piedmont, more local meetings were established.

In 1757, while visiting coastal Quakers, John Woolman, a Quaker minister, sent a letter to Cane Creek (and New Garden Meeting) concerning enslavement. He advised that, as they settled into their new lives, they should "consider the force of your examples, and think how much your successors may be thereby affected." Their customs should be "agreeable to sound wisdom." In short, be aware that others are watching how you treat bondswomen and men.[87]

Newly convinced Quaker and land speculator Herman Husband (or Husbands) had recently moved from Maryland into the area. Settling some twenty miles southwest of Cane Creek Meeting, he soon joined the meeting. Bothered by the enslavement he witnessed on a business trip to the Caribbean and the enslaved his father owned, he presciently warned that slavery was on the rise in the Piedmont. While lamenting the ill treatment of Blacks, he also saw two other emerging problems resulting from enslavement. First, as Quakers enslaved more Blacks, decadence replaced Quaker simplicity. Ending enslavement would encourage more industry from Quakers and less dependence on their enslaved. His second complaint against slavery was more selfish: increased enslavement meant fewer white workers who could earn money and thus purchase land from him.[88]

By the early 1800s, the problem of Quakers and their enslaved may have been all but nonexistent. Quaker minister Stephen Grellet traveled the Piedmont area twice, first in 1800 and then in 1809. While he visited all the Quaker meetings in this area on both missions, enslavement was not mentioned in his recollections of North Carolina. It is telling that, after leaving North Carolina in 1800, he journeyed into Tennessee and then back into Virginia, where he lamented that slaves, who were "ragged and emaciated," were treated cruelly.[89]

There were few enslaved around Snow Camp—thus a blasé attitude toward the plight of the enslaved emerged. When asked by the North Carolina Yearly Meeting to select a committee to explore ways to help the enslaved in 1800, no committee was formed in Cane Creek. In 1809, the Yearly Meeting, concerned about its "Free Negro" efforts, inquired about opinions, and Cane Creek bluntly stated the program should end. While seemingly apathetic to the cause, in 1798 a Cane Creek committee confronted a father and son who were involved in the slave trade. In 1846, a woman was disowned for holding and selling enslaved people.[90]

Perhaps because of Cane Creek's apathy concerning the enslaved, some members participated in the URR, which ran through the Cane Creek area. Member and wagonmaker Frederic Stafford may have built false-bottomed wagons used in the URR. He moved west to Guilford County, and since this was nearer to New Garden Meeting, the center of the URR, perhaps there was a growing need for such equipment. Still, frustrated that their fellow members weren't involved enough in the abolition of enslavement, a few Cane Creek members helped establish the ardently abolitionist Freedom's Hill Wesleyan Church a mile south of the Meeting in 1848.[91]

The thirty-mile trek to Cane Creek Meeting led to Quakers in Guilford County requesting meeting status from Cane Creek in 1751, and this was finalized in 1754. Weeks states that "New Garden was destined to become the most important meeting in the State [*sic*], and it was the mother of many others." No doubt much of this acclaim came because of the Coffin family, leaders in the URR, who were members of New Garden. Nantucket antislavery Quakers had settled around New Garden, and in 1767, the meeting faced a dilemma: Should it receive Obadiah Harris from Virginia, who had sold a slave, which made him a participant in enslavement, no matter his motive? Known also for his drinking habit, after confessing his sins, Harris was admitted. Nearly two decades later, Bolin Clark of Tom's Creek Preparative Meeting was complained of by New Garden Meeting for releasing his enslaved only to sell them. Like Harris, he addressed this fault and then purchased them back. Perhaps this staunch stance against enslavement stemmed from New Garden's beginnings in the home of Thomas Beals, an ardent foe of enslavement. Disapproving of the continued presence of slavery in North Carolina, as the century closed out, Beals led an exodus of New Garden members to what he termed the "promised land" of the West.[92]

Roughly midway between Cane Creek and New Garden, a group of Quakers who had been meeting in homes sought preparative meeting status from New Garden Meeting in 1755, which was granted in 1757. These Friends, mostly from Pennsylvania but also from Virginia and eventually from Nantucket as well, became a monthly meeting in 1773. Centre Meeting, the initial home of the North Carolina Manumission Society, seemed stalwart against enslavement; Daniel Worth grew up a member of Centre and later moved to Indiana in 1822. He was one of the initial founders of the staunchly abolitionist Wesleyan Church. Armed with copies of Hinton Rowan Helper's incendiary pamphlet *The Impending Crisis of the South* as well as other antislavery literature, Worth illegally distributed the material throughout North Carolina. He was tried and convicted of his deeds and, out of jail on bond while awaiting an appeal, fled to Indiana.[93]

This strong legacy against enslavement continued in the early 1800s, when the North Carolina Manumission Society was formed. Six members from New Garden attended the initial meeting of the Society at Centre Friends Meeting: Benjamin Hiatt, Tristram Coffin, Bethuel Coffin, Isaac Gardner, Henry Ballinger, and Paul Macy. Benajah Hiatt and Jeremiah Hubbard took the message of manumission out to other denominations.[94]

STATE of NORTH-CAROLINA,
Randolph COUNTY.

This Indenture,

MADE the 3rd Day of May in the Year of our Lord one thousand eight hundred and thirteen between Zebedee Wood Chairman of the county court of Randolph county and State aforesaid, on behalf of the Justices of the said county and their Successors, of the one Part, and William Dennis of the other Part, WITNESSETH, That the said Zebedee Wood in pursuance to an order of the said county court, made the 3rd day of May and according to the directions of the Act of Assembly in that case made and provided, doth put, place and bind unto the said William Dennis a boy of Colour ~~an Orphan~~, named George Newby — now of the age of Twelve years, with the said William to live after the manner of an apprentice and servant, until the said apprentice shall attain to the age of twenty one years: during all which time the said apprentice his master faithfully shall serve, his lawful commands every where readily obey: he shall not at any time absent himself from his said master's service without leave, but in all things as a good and faithful servant shall behave towards his said master. And the said William Dennis doth covenant, promise and agree to and with the said Zebedee Wood that he will teach and instruct, or cause to be taught and instructed, the said George Newby to learn the potters trade and that he will constantly find and provide for the said apprentice, during the term aforesaid, sufficient diet, washing, lodging and apparel, fitting for an apprentice; and also all other things necessary, both in sickness and in health.

IN WITNESS WHEREOF, the parties to these presents have interchangeably set their hands and seals, the day and year first above written.

Signed, sealed, and delivered in the presence of

Zebedee Wood (Seal)
Wm Dennis (Seal)

Indenture certificate of George Newby. Randolph County Apprentice Bonds: George Newby, 1813. CR.081.101.2. *State Archives of North Carolina.*

Unlike some other Quaker meetings, no members of Centre were disowned for any acts related to the peculiar institution. In 1813, member William Dennis, who opposed enslavement and worked within the Manumission Society, apprenticed a young Black boy, George Newby, in the family pottery business. This was possibly part of an initiative by local Quakers to take in children of freed slaves and provide them an education. Members collected money to fund sending slaves back to Africa, but the captain of the ship instead took them to the Caribbean and sold them back into slavery. One of these slaves wrote to the meeting and asked that this process be stopped. The first North Carolina Manumission Society session was held at Centre, whose members were major leaders in this movement. Member Seth Beeson Hockett regularly went to Indiana to visit his sisters, and he hid slaves in a false-bottomed wagon on these journeys. Andy Murrow, an orphan raised by abolitionist Joshua Stanley, was part of the URR. His particular station was at the intersection of U.S. 220 and N.C. 62, not far from Centre. It is believed that other members of Centre were also active in the URR.[95]

FARTHER WEST OF CENTRE, Deep River Friends Meeting began in 1753 on the forks of Deep River, in present-day southwest Guilford County, near Forsyth County, becoming a preparative meeting in 1758. It was "one of the strongest monthly meetings" in the Piedmont. Like New Garden Meeting, most of its early members were from Philadelphia and Nantucket. Deep River disowned one member who harbored and concealed a bondsman. Phebe Wall's family were founding members of Deep River. She married non-Quaker John Haley but oddly was not disowned for this union. As evidenced in his will read in 1813, he enslaved four Blacks. Some circumstances were not as clear. Jonathan and Louisa Harris may have owned slaves or housed freed slaves.[96]

In 1816, Deep River Meeting was the other major location for the North Carolina Manumission Society. Thirty-one Deep River members were involved in the Manumission Society. This may have led to further disownments, including Joseph and Mary Burcham, for hiring enslaved people from other enslavers. In 1819, Deep River also disowned William Bard Jr. In 1825, member George Mendenhall was disowned for marrying outside of the Quakers and for "deviating from plainness in dress and address." One of the consistent complaints of Quakers concerning slave ownership was that it led to a lavish lifestyle, often manifested in fancy dress. This may or may not have been so with Mendenhall, who trained his slaves in various skills and then transported them to free states. The last of his enslaved were manumitted in 1864. Abigail Mendenhall taught freedmen in a house on her land. One Deep River member was disowned for enslaving one person, and interestingly, one was disowned for "harboring and concealing a slave." Still, like other meetings, officially, Deep River Meeting was neither involved in nor condoned the URR.[97]

Spring Friends Meeting originated from Cane Creek Meeting and was formally recognized in 1773, although Friends had met at "the spring" at least a decade earlier. Interestingly, while roughly nine miles east of Cane Creek Meeting on today's Greensboro/Chapel Hill Road, there is no indication that it was part of any URR activities. Some members were disowned for enslavement: David Cloud in 1815, William Lindley in 1828, and Oliver Newlin in 1842. Ironically, Oliver's father, John, lobbied the North Carolina General Assembly to legislate ways to make it easier for citizens to manumit their enslaved. The family of John W. Woody recalls their grandfather sought homes in Ohio for his enslaved. Other members fought against enslavement. In 1784, William Lindley was placed in charge of the Book of Manumissions. In 1800, a committee was formed to investigate how Friends treated their slaves. In 1808, another committee was formed "to have under their care all suffering cases of people of colour that now or have been under Friends care." John Newlin was a member of the North Carolina Manumission Society.[98]

Quaker settlers just outside of present-day High Point informally began meeting for worship in 1773, and by, 1780 Deep River Meeting recognized Springfield Preparative Meeting. Interestingly, tired of the South Carolina slave society, many members from Bush River Meeting in South Carolina moved to Springfield beginning in 1803. Springfield member Nathan Hunt broke from typical Quaker measured expression and reticence and expressed strong abolitionist feelings to the meeting. Criticized for his forceful opinions, he once preached that "he would as soon as hear an ass bray as to hear a slaveowner preach the Gospel." He also led the "Free Produce" movement whereby Quakers could purchase items and food not produced by the enslaved rather than reward enslavers for the unpaid labors of their chattel. Member Allen Thomlinson's farm might have been a station on the URR. It is believed that a large rock marked the location of his farm for runaways.[99]

Rock marker that pointed to an URR refuge near Springfield Meeting, High Point, North Carolina. Museum of Old Domestic Life. *By the author.*

Enslavement was a divisive practice, yet manumitting bondspeople brought on economic trials. John Carter's family, tired of the stress, headed to the West from Springfield in the early 1800s, but his son Samuel, an enslaver, stayed behind. When Nancy Holton's father released the enslaved inherited from the family, he had to buckle down to fill the labor void and "win the necessities and comforts of life." Solomon Blair boldly defied strict state prohibitions concerning educating the enslaved. He secretly taught them, and his reputation among Blacks was remembered as "superb."[100]

Westfield Friends Meeting, established in 1787, soon "became the center of a large and important Quaker community" in Surry County. One of the founding members of Westfield Meeting, Joseph Jessup, originally from Perquimans and Carteret Counties, finally settled on the banks of the Dan River in Surry County in 1783. He built a plantation and a mill that his family continued to run for years. His was the only enslaving Quaker family in Surry County. It is not clear if Joseph enslaved Blacks, but two of his sons, Elijah and Caleb, owned at least one apiece. His other son, William, enslaved fifteen Blacks as of 1816, when he deeded them over to the North Carolina Yearly Meeting. It is not known how these sons acquired their enslaved. It is possible they worked on the plantation and at the mill. It is also possible they belonged to their wives. Curiously, while Westfield Friends Meeting disowned many members for marrying outside of the Quaker community, they did not disown any of these members for enslaving others.[101]

Deep Creek Meeting and Hunting Creek Meeting, established in the late 1700s in the Upper Yadkin River Valley, were no strangers to the peculiar institution. Some enslaving members farmed this region, which included several large enslaving plantations. Blacks from Guinea were abundant in the area. Quakers often inherited enslaved people, and these were retained in a "protective custody" manner, much like the Quaker "Free Negroes," which are discussed later. Within this small enclave of western North Carolina Quakers, the Wales family was known for its strict views against enslavement. At the same time, one Wales family's hearth featured andirons crafted with stylized Black heads on them. Deep Creek member Strangeman Hutchins was complained of for enslavement. In 1779, he offered a paper to the meeting whereby he apologized. In 1814, Quaker children who attended a local school were mocked by students from enslaving families. Ironically, many of the enslaving families were in fact quite poor.[102]

The Piedmont culture was not as dependent on enslavement as the coastal regions. Farmers in the immediate area around Snow Camp enslaved few if any Blacks, but the region west of Snow Camp was no stranger to enslavement. German Lutherans settled to the west and north, and many of these families were enslavers. Several large farms, some over one thousand acres, were worked by enslaved people. North of this area in the small mill village of Alamance, as early as the 1830s, Edwin Michael Holt owned enough land to be considered a planter, and in 1860 he owned one thousand acres and enslaved fifty-one Blacks. Likewise, Scottish Presbyterians had settled north and east of Snow Camp, and many of them owned slaves.[103]

In Guilford County, about one-third of the residents did not enslave others, and enslavement was much less prevalent among Quakers in this area than on the East Coast. In 1781, following the lead of the North Carolina Yearly Meeting, the Western Quarterly Meeting addressed Friends in the backcountry of North Carolina concerning enslavement. If, after these enslavers were approached by fellow Quakers who tried to convince them of their "iniquity," they still refused to release their slaves, they were to be disowned. In 1783, the Yearly Meeting pointedly recommended that monthly meetings disown slaveholding members. In 1787, the Western Quarterly Meeting followed suit.[104]

Still, despite the threat of disownment, some Quakers resisted manumission well into the 1800s. The issue was cultural, social, and political. After the American Revolution, states sought to embody the freedom and liberty that was fought for. Beginning in 1777 and continuing into the 1800s, Northern states began the process of eliminating enslavement. Vermont and Massachusetts passed laws ending enslavement; Pennsylvania, Rhode Island, and New Hampshire preferred gradual emancipation. New York and New Jersey then followed suit. Virginia even legalized private manumission of the enslaved in 1782. In 1794, George Washington introduced a petition from New England Quakers that demanded an end to the international enslavement trade. The Constitution as adopted by the states would outlaw the slave *trade* in 1808, and this brought hopes of ending enslavement altogether. Thus, for a brief time, there was a widespread feeling that enslavement in America was near an end. It cannot be a coincidence that this was the same time Quakers were calling on fellow members to manumit their bondspeople. So, why did the problem of enslavement continue among North Carolina Quakers?[105]

There were many rebellions instigated by the enslaved in the 1790s, the most important of which was the Haitian Revolution in the colony of Saint-Domingue in Hispaniola, led by Toussaint L'Ouverture. Slave rebellions in Louisiana, Cuba, and Puerto Rico, among others, also occurred. In the United States, there were increasing fears of insurrections by the enslaved, especially in Virginia. Gabriel's Rebellion in Virginia in 1800 was the last straw. Southern Republicans now agreed with Northern Federalists that "too much preaching of liberty and equality undermined the institution of slavery." Talk of manumission, gradual or instantaneous, had to end. Sadly, enslavement was used to quell the Black population from further revolts.

Thus, by the end of the 1700s into the 1800s, especially in the South, there was a decline in manumissions; the end of racial mingling, including religious meetings; the reemergence of Black Codes; and the legislation of severe punishments for fugitives. Beginning in 1806, Southern states declared that free Blacks were no longer welcome. Finally, Southerners, afraid of the rise of capitalism in the North, fell back on the labors of the enslaved to retain their agricultural economy and thus their power in the fledgling nation.

And the only way to justify this resort back to enslavement was to insist on the inferiority of Blacks, resulting in paternalistic ownership. As Gordon Wood points out, Southerners "began to suggest that the characteristics of the African slaves might be innate and that in some basic sense they were designed for slavery." Therefore, "slaves had no inherent capacity for freedom it was said, and thus the slaveholders had a Christian and patriarchal responsibility to hold them in bondage and look after them." These beliefs were not foreign to North Carolina Quakers, and they spawned the very questions that emerged in the continued Quaker debate over enslavement.[106]

In 1803, traveling Quaker Zachariah Dicks left Guilford County for an extended preaching tour of Southern Friends meetings where he denounced enslavement and warned of repercussions if they tolerated the institution. Quaker minister William Forster visited meetings just west of New Garden in 1824. In his journal, he wrote, "We see but little of slaves in these parts of the state, no more than if we were in Pennsylvania." While this observation can be taken as a sign of Quaker objections to slavery, it still reveals that, after the North Carolina Yearly Meeting demanded that Quaker enslavers be disowned, the practice was still intact. Indeed, the Discipline of 1854 demanded that Quakers who persisted in enslaving Blacks should be disowned.[107]

QUAKERS AGAINST QUAKERS

These are the reasons why we are against the traffic of men-body, as followeth: is there any that would be done or handled in this manner? viz., to be sold or made a slave for all the time of his life?
—Minutes of Germantown Meeting, Pennsylvania, 1688

Slavery is a curse to the whites as well as to the blacks. It makes the white fathers cruel, and sensual; the sons violent and licentious; it contaminates the daughters, and makes the wives wretched.
—Harriet Jacobs, former North Carolina enslaved, writing as Linda Brent, Incidents in the Life of a Slave Girl *(1845), 53*

Quaker minister John Woolman (1720–1772) described himself as a "poor, unlearned working man of New Jersey" who was raised on a plantation. At the age of twenty-three, his employer, a shopkeeper and baker, asked him to finalize a bill of sale for a "negro woman" to another Quaker. The incident struck a nerve in Woolman and awakened him to the plight of the enslaved. "I was so afflicted in my mind, that I said, before my master and the Friend that I believed slave-keeping a practice inconsistent with the Christian religion." He knew that other members of the meeting were enslavers. More specifically, the New Jersey town of Perth Amboy, which lay near Woolman's home, imported slaves who then were housed in barracks.[108]

In 1746, Woolman and a friend set out on a preaching tour that led them from New Jersey down into Virginia, ending in Perquimans in North Carolina. Looking back on that travel, especially his time in Perquimans, his observations reveal two concerns relating to the slaves and their owners:

> *When I ate, drank and lodged free-cost with people who lived in ease on the hard labor of their slaves I felt uneasy.... Where the masters bore a good share of the burden, and lived frugally, so that their servants were provided for, and their labor moderate, I felt more easy; but where they lived in a more costly way, and laid heavy burdens on their slaves, my exercise was great and I frequently had conversations with them in private concerning it.*[109]

One observation from Woolman's recollections is a distinction of Black bondsmen and women: for Woolman, those who were worked hard for the reward of their masters were termed "slaves," while those treated well were deemed "servants." Thus, Woolman's conscience is less disturbed with "servants" around him than when enslaved are in service. Is it the blatant disparity between masters who are well-to-do and their enslaved who are mistreated that stirs his conscience? Quakers defied social class distinctions, so this might indicate the Quaker preference for the equality of all people. But at this time in North Carolina, the social distinction between white and Black, servant and enslaved, was becoming more pronounced. In essence, the Quaker belief in the equality of all people was being undermined by the institution of enslavement.

While no doubt concerned about the plight of the enslaved, Woolman seems more distressed over the spiritual and moral direction of the Southern slave culture.

> *This trade of importing slaves from their native country being much encouraged amongst them and the white people and their children so generally living without labor, was frequently the subject of my serious thoughts. I saw in these southern provinces so many vices and corruptions, increased by this trade and this life, that it appeared to me as a dark gloominess hanging over the land; and though now many willingly run into it, yet in future the consequence will be grievous to posterity.*[110]

This distinction between the treatment of the enslaved in the North and in the South is curious. Woolman was raised and worked in the Hudson Valley,

John Woolman. Original sepia drawing probably by his friend Robert Smith III. *Wikimedia Commons.*

a region that included Perth Amboy. This area, especially in New York City (originally New Amsterdam) was heavily influenced by Dutch economic culture. David Fischer concludes that "Dutch slavery in the Hudson Valley was a cruel and brutal business, as bondage was in most times and places." But it wasn't until 1774 that New York Quakers "condemned the buying and selling of slaves by members of the Society of Friends." Woolman could not have been a stranger to enslavement.[111]

Curiously, spurred by his brief tour of North Carolina, Woolman penned his thoughts on the matter, which were eventually published by (enslaver) Benjamin Franklin in 1754. What was it about *Southern* enslavement, particularly in Perquimans, North Carolina, that led to Woolman's "unease"? As we have seen, Northerners treated their slaves just as harshly as Southerners. How was enslavement in North Carolina so different from the treatment of other slaves that Woolman was inspired to publish a tract about the matter?

Historian Gordon Wood, examining the important transitions taking place in America between 1789 and 1815, provides a sobering answer. As previously noted, in Rhode Island the Narragansett Planters emulated the ostentatious lifestyle of Southern planters. Such a mindset was quite different from that of the normal economic, societal, and political culture of the North. As the North came to value paid labor for all social ranks, "much of the white population of the South was becoming more and more contemptuous of work and desirous of acquiring the leisure that slavery seemed to offer." In essence, the divide between what Wood describes as "an industrious North and a lethargic South" was emerging. And on top of it all, this Southern *slave* culture was breeding the deferential society that the original Quakers sought to end.[112]

Woolman was not the only Quaker in the South to notice this disturbing trend. Herman Husband, one of the key leaders of the North Carolina Regulators movement in the Piedmont area, grew up on his father's plantation in Maryland in the 1720s and 1730s. His father guided him toward the genteel life of a planter. Raised an Anglican yet taught a strict form of piety by his grandfather, Husband began questioning the culture of ease, luxury, and indulgence along with stark class divisions of Maryland.

He wrestled with these two ways of life for many years. Inspired by Quaker Robert Barclay's *An Apology for the True Christian Divinity*, he converted to the Quaker faith and assumed their call for frugality and their refusal to honor class distinctions that were reinforced by the emerging gentlemen plantation society.

Quakers were known for their economic prowess, and Husband had high aspirations of success as a land prospector. Yet he also recognized that enslavement was affecting whites in general and Quakers in particular. Quakers were becoming lax in their spiritual discipline and changing to a life of ease. After he moved to North Carolina, he instantly recognized that enslavement was becoming more of a problem not just on the coast but in the Piedmont as well, changing the way people worked and lived. Ever the strict Quaker disciplinarian, he worried about and fought against this culture that, in his view, threatened the very heart of Quakerism.[113]

These conflicting thoughts came together when Husband moved to North Carolina in 1755 to set up his land-speculating business. And this intricate web of competing principles and aspirations was at the heart of the overall problem of Quakers as they wrestled with their rising dependence on the enslaved.

Interestingly, Woolman describes a personal tension concerning enslavement that reveals a telling Quaker trait: Should industrious Quakers follow conscience or vocation? Overall, we see that, in Woolman's case, his lucrative vocation gave way to his religious scruples while other Quakers put vocation before conscience with regards to slavery. Was this tension of vocation over conscience what caught his eye concerning enslavement in North Carolina?

We find a clue to Woolman's dilemma when, concerning the year 1756, he writes of two things: his worries over the "state of churches [Quaker meetings] in our southern provinces" and his successful retail business, which required much of his time and led to lucrative sales of products that were, in his growing estimation, frivolous and thus unnecessary. We see a veiled reference to the life of enslavers in Woolman's journal:

> *Did those who have the care of great estates attend with singleness of heart to this heavenly Instructor, which so opens and enlarges the mind as to cause men to love their neighbors as themselves, they would have wisdom given to them to manage their concerns, without employing some people in providing the luxuries of life, or others in laboring too hard; but for want of steadily regarding this principle of Divine love, a selfish*

spirit takes place in the minds of people which is attended with darkness and manifold confusions in the world.[114]

In 1757, Woolman, beginning in Maryland, again headed to the South, where the "gain of oppression"—that is, the fruits of enslaved labor—confronted him as he lodged with various hosts. Rather than eat and rest free in the homes of enslaving Friends, he offered, at the risk of offense, to pay the enslaved for their labors: "offering them [money] to some who appeared to be wealthy people was a trial to both me and them." It is often pointed out by historians that Woolman refused to eat the produce of slaves, a belief that was called "free produce or "free labor."[115]

Important for this study is Woolman's 1757 "Epistle to the Piedmont Quaker Meetings," Cane Creek and New Garden, both not even ten years old. Cane Creek members had ties to the Perquimans Meeting, so perhaps Woolman became aware of their particular situation from discussions with his coastal hosts. From such discussions he was privy to the changes that Husband warned of. Sticking to the coast, Woolman did not visit these meetings, but he noted that they were "amongst the first planters in one part of a province" who were "improving a wilderness." He reminded them that they should set a good example for those who settled after them. That example included frugality attained through honest labor. "I have been informed that there is a large number of Friends in your parts who have no slaves," implying that some Friends in the Piedmont were enslavers. He urges the two meetings to refrain from purchasing slaves, but he did not request that they manumit them. "Follow in simplicity that body of exercise, that plainness and frugality, which true wisdom leads to; so you may be preserved from those dangers which attend such as are aiming at outward ease and greatness." In other words, don't be like the Quakers in the eastern part of North Carolina who have become reliant on slaves.[116]

In the sixth month of 1757, Woolman left the Virginia Yearly Meeting and traveled back to North Carolina. On the journey, he was joined by some Friends from New Garden Meeting. Perhaps they discussed enslavement in general among colonial Friends. Woolman then attended the Simon's (Symonds) Creek Meeting, where he was greatly troubled by a dilemma. At the meeting, a member who had arrived home from visiting New Garden Meeting and who also was an enslaver, expressed concern about "Friends so much neglecting their duty in the education of slaves." A suggestion was made about "having meetings sometimes appointed for them on a week-day." Curiously, there was no decision against slavery itself.[117]

In 1764, Woolman attended the Yearly Meeting in Philadelphia. In his *Journal*, he records the speech of an elderly Quaker minister who lamented the demise of Quaker values due to their increase in wealth. Sixty years earlier, Friends were "plain, lowly minded people," and "tenderness and contrition" was manifest in their meeting. Twenty years later, Friends had increased in wealth and were conforming to the fashions of the world, losing their previous humility. And the trend was worse in the present day. These were the very points that Woolman had preached continually concerning the use of slaves. Woolman writes in his *Journal*, "The way of living and the annual expenses of some of them are such that it seems impracticable for them to set their slaves free without changing their own way of life."[118]

While in North Carolina, Woolman would have been aware of Perquimans Quaker Thomas Newby, who enslaved fourteen humans and was a successful merchant. His will reveals a vast assortment of items indicative of an affluent lifestyle. Likewise, Quaker cabinetmaker and businessman John Sanders, who enslaved eleven people, was quite successful, as was evident in his substantial lavish holdings in the mid- to late 1700s. Similarly, Quaker Thomas White owned twenty-six bondspeople who no doubt led to White's extreme wealth. These Quakers would have been considered "Albemarle Elites" and were no doubt the epitome of Woolman's "unease."[119]

Thus, while slavery was very much on Woolman's mind, its effect on Quaker spirituality and simplicity was just as important if not more. Nearly a century later, Linda Brent/Harriet Jacobs wrote, "Slavery is a curse to the whites as well as to the blacks. It makes the white fathers cruel, and sensual; the sons violent and licentious; it contaminates the daughters, and makes the wives wretched." Quakers, despite their incremental snail's pace of change, were ahead of the matter by one hundred years. Still, in Woolman's time, we see the beginnings of a tripartite approach to the dilemma of slavery within the ranks of the North Carolina Quakers: Oppressive bondage is not correct, Black slaves/servants receiving humane treatment is tolerable but not preferable, and total freedom is preferred. Herman Husband added one more worry: with the increase of slavery, the white man's ability to purchase more land and tools and barns to improve himself was diminishing.[120]

John Woolman's 1757 conversations in the Albemarle region, specifically with Simon's Creek and Piney Woods Meetings as well as individuals, no doubt spurred much introspection and soul-searching concerning enslavement but ultimately led to little action. Still, Quaker leaders of Pennsylvania were increasingly convinced that enslavement among Friends must end, and their influence was trickling down to the Albemarle Quakers. One Quaker, Thomas Nicholson of Perquimans Meeting, served on a committee with Woolman while visiting the Yearly Meeting in Pennsylvania in 1757. Afterward, Nicholson corresponded regularly with the Pennsylvania leaders, and in 1767, he penned a letter to North Carolina Friends in which he, like Woolman, emphasized the negative effects that enslavement brought both to Quaker enslavers and to their enslaved. He had "for many Years been distressed in my mind on account of Negroes remaining Slaves in our Society for several Reasons," which he then enumerated.[121]

Nicholson boldly stated that the slave trade was a "very wicked and abominable Practice" that was "contrary to the natural Rights and Privileges of all mankind" and violated the Golden Rule. Derisively referring to enslaving Friends as minors, he claimed that enslavement was a "Snare to Friends' children, by being made use of as Nurseries to Pride, Idleness and a Lording Spirit over our Fellow Creatures." He then addressed the "contrary Behavior" of enslaved peoples that provoked "anger Passion and unsavory Expressions" from their masters and mistresses. Further, he asserted that enslavement was a "Contradiction to our Principle and Testimony against wars and Fighting," meaning the tactics of wars to capture Africans and the potential of the enslaved rising up against their masters. Curiously, he also noted that efforts to "inculcate Principles of true Religion Piety and Virtue" had resulted in "but a small effect" on the enslaved, thus "the Seeds of Discontent and uneasiness remain under a Sense of their State of Bondage."[122]

Given these conditions, Nicholson then writes that "any thoughtful person" who possessed "mostly by inheritance and breeding in their Families" eighteen to twenty bondswomen and men "must sympathize with me in my Distress of mind." While encouraging "Friends to discourage the practice as much as possible," he still retains the manner of a gradual manumission of the enslaved "on reasonable lawful terms." Taking a stand as an example to his fellow Friends, he says he will release his slaves (he owned five). But if there is no clear "Method" by which to manumit slaves then "there is nothing that appears to me to be more safe and expedient in the present Distress than for those that have them (that are willing to live with them and behave themselves well) to keep them and use them well" so that "after a reasonable number of Years of Servitude" proceeds from their labor can be used to "make them free under proper Guardians and restrictions to keep them from becoming a public Charge or Offense to Government." Those who "behave badly, and are not content to live with their Masters or Mistresses," were "to be sold to other masters or mistresses" as long as a proper (caring) owner could be located.[123]

This was the very definition of what scholars today call "gradual manumission."

As North Carolina Quakers struggled over their approaches to free their enslaved, the debate ultimately came down to one issue: Should they take a more measured, thoughtful course of gradual manumission (gradualism), as suggested by Nicholson, or should they advocate for immediate emancipation and thus abolition (immediatism)? One lone voice among the coastal Quakers advocated vehemently for the latter.

George Walton was a successful merchant in Perquimans County who also owned land and enslaved at least one Black. His second wife, Mary, was from the Quaker Newby family, and in order for her to remain in good standing in her meeting, George converted to her faith and was confirmed a Quaker in 1773. He quickly became involved in the manumission movement and soon was leading the charge for antislavery among North Carolina Quakers. The fire that sparked his motivation was a sequence of dreams he had beginning in December 1772 and into 1773. He interpreted these dreams as his call to fight against enslavement. Michael Crawford points out that Walton's campaign coincided as "agitation of the issue of slaveholding was reaching a pivotal juncture in the affairs of the North Carolina Yearly Meeting."[124]

In April 1774, Thomas Newby, "uneasy" about his enslavement of Blacks, followed Quaker protocol and asked Perquimans Meeting for permission to release his bondsmen and women. The request went to the Yearly Meeting, which decided that he could do so with his local meeting's permission. The local meeting withheld permission while a committee explored the several ramifications involved. First, could the manumitted person support him/herself upon freedom? Second, the rising tensions between the colonies and Britain led to fears that the British would incite the enslaved to revolt or even join the British ranks. Last, the real problem to be considered was simple enough: It was against North Carolina law to manumit any enslaved person. Quaker principles, as prescribed in the Bible, required them to follow all laws. Manumission meant breaking the law. On top of that, if Newby released his enslaved, then, by law, they could be rounded up and resold back into servitude. As the local meeting seemingly dawdled, "Newby continued to own slaves and his conscience remained troubled."[125]

It was at this same time that Walton began in earnest to promote abolition. That summer he wrote Newby a letter in which he encouraged Newby to release his slaves immediately in order to relieve his "unease." Putting conscience above citizenship, Walton wrote, "Some may be ready to say the Law is against our Seting [*sic*] them free, So that if we are willing the law wont [*sic*] let us. But know this O Man whoe'er thou art the law of God is not to be Subject to the law of Man, if contrary to truth & holiness." To buttress his argument, he cited the biblical story of Daniel, who stood against the decrees of the Persian King Darius.[126]

The following year, just after the colony increased slave patrols, the North Carolina Yearly Meeting, no doubt spurred by Walton's war against enslavement, declared that enslaving was inconsistent with Quaker discipline and that all members should rid themselves of all aspects of enslavement as soon as possible. In March 1776, just months before the thirteen colonies declared their independence from Britain, Thomas Newby finally manumitted his enslaved people. Pushed by Walton, fourteen others from the Perquimans Meeting also freed their enslaved. In just a few months, forty or more enslaved Blacks were free. Not everyone in the meetings was convinced. "Other Quakers were sympathetic but hesitant, and still others were unwilling." The North Carolina General Assembly, again in fear that those manumitted would, at the direction of the British, foment a rebellion, condemned these Quaker actions and quickly enacted laws in 1777 authorizing the capture and resale of manumitted Blacks. Sadly, that same year, the North Carolina Yearly Meeting noted that all bondspeople who had been released had been captured and resold or they hid in fear while hunters and vigilantes searched for them. The good intentions of the Quakers produced the very thing they were meant to end.[127]

Tired of North Carolina's continued efforts to thwart the Quakers' manumission of their enslaved, increasingly defiant against the laws enacted as part of this effort, and perhaps inspired by George Walton, Thomas Nicholson reversed course in 1775. He buttressed his new opinion with a long list of Bible passages. Nicholson further argued that Quakers who accept laws allowing the manumission of their enslaved based only on "Meritorious causes" or laws that allow for the sale of bondspeople "without paying regard to a tender Scruple of Conscience" simply continue to condone and participate in the institution of enslavement. Further, Nicholson then asserted that Quakers who don't manumit their enslaved ignore their guilt of conscience, thus sinning rather than being free of sin.[128]

Thus, Nicholson boldly and naively insisted that Quakers must manumit their enslaved immediately and then let the chips, no matter how cruel, fall where they may because "we have faith to believe, that the God whom we endeavor to serve is able to preserve those whom we do set free, from falling into the hands of cruel and wicked Men." Having thus washed his hands of "that cruel Babylonish Practice" of gradual manumission, his conscience was now clear from any guilt whatsoever. And despite all the setbacks and the consequent potential harm to those manumitted, Quakers defied the laws of North Carolina and released their enslaved peoples.[129]

Quaker slaveholders in Perquimans and Pasquotank were now between a rock and hard place. Clear one's conscience and risk the former enslaved's life or have the enslaved continue to live on his/her land under a kind of bond of protection. Such former enslaved could also hire themselves out to earn extra money. In exchange, the white farmer provided some form of protection for the worker. But even this was not safe. In 1790, Quaker Thomas Prichard enslaved twenty-eight bondspeople. He manumitted one, Thomas Pritchet, but allowed him to stay on the plantation and work a piece of his land, somewhat like sharecropping. The formerly enslaved Pritchet became a successful farmer. But Prichard died, and his wife then married Holland Lockwood. It is not clear what transpired between the two, but Holland threatened to deport Pritchet if he did not work for him. Pritchet left his wife and fled for Virginia.[130]

Quaker Joseph Nicholson released Jacob Nicholson, who continued living on the Nicholson farm. But soon slave catchers pursued him so intensely that he fled, leaving behind "a mother, a child and two brothers." Thomas Nicholson released Jupiter, whose wife was also freed by Quaker Gabriel Cosand. Jupiter worked as a seaman for two years before the slave catchers caught up to him. He fled for Virginia, leaving behind his family, who were then captured and re-enslaved.[131]

Sadly, while Perquimans, Pasquotank, and Chowan Quakers somewhat selfishly cleared their consciences from what they called "the gain of oppression," 134 of their released enslaved were rounded up and sold back into slavery by 1792. Walton's dream-inspired insistence on immediate emancipation and Nicholson's later switch from gradual manumission to absolute abolition were altruistic catalysts to relieve the "unease" of

Quaker enslavers. Ultimately, however, it wound up costing the formerly enslaved their freedom, including the five released by Nicholson to clear his conscience.[132]

QUAKER HISTORIAN THOMAS HAMM observes that in 1800, "American Friends were a united group, bound together by a common heritage, by intervisitation and communication, and by a common set of rules and values." No doubt some of this cohesiveness was rooted in the debate on enslavement. In the 1800s, however, the Friends endured several divisions, the most significant of which was the Hicksite Separation, which rocked the Quakers in the 1820s. This division directly affected the Quaker deliberations over enslavement in North Carolina.[133]

Elias Hicks (1748–1830) was a highly respected Quaker minister who lived on Long Island. In his later years, he suddenly professed, in often contradictory ways, doctrines counter to those of his day. Worried, like Woolman and Husband, that Friends were becoming too worldly as they succeeded in their industry, and frustrated that they were adopting the religious ideas of non-Quakers (there was a huge evangelical revival running throughout the new nation), Hicks, around 1819, sought to bring Quakers back to what he saw as their roots.

The Hicksites, "a diverse, if not motley group," soon divided over three reform movements in the 1830s—antislavery, women's rights, and nonresistance—all of which were important to groups of progressively disparate Friends. One-third of the members of the American Anti-Slavery Society, formed in 1833, were Quakers, and most of those were Hicksites. However, many Hicksites were opposed to the radical beliefs and tactics of antislavery associations, and Quakers overall, like many others at that time, were afraid of radicals and emerging feminists.[134]

Elias Hicks emerged as a strong abolitionist voice among Quakers. After touring Maryland and Virginia, first in 1798 and later in 1813, he began a vociferous and protracted attack on the institution of enslavement. His vitriol caused a split among Quakers known as the Hicksite Split. The Hicksites favored strict abolitionism, which, more and more, had become so radical that it was now encouraging violence. Orthodox Quakers were antislavery, but as typical for traditional Quakers, they were anti-violence.[135]

North Carolina Quakers remained Orthodox as opposed to Hicksite. If the Hicksites favored strict abolitionism, one reason the North Carolina

Friends may have remained in the Orthodox camp was to avoid the adamant call for immediate manumission and the end of enslavement and even condemn the radical tactics of abolitionists. Choosing instead to follow proper Quaker social decorum and not risk the wrath of fellow Friends or their enslaving neighbors, they would not adopt the radical stance of the Hicksites in regard to enslavement.[136]

By the 1840s, as Black bondage became even more entrenched in Southern society, the major religions of the nation had split over the issue of enslavement. From this division emerged the Methodist Episcopal Church, a pro-slavery denomination that validated the institution of enslavement rather than confront it. In 1845, one daring congregation in Jamestown refused to join the Methodist Episcopal Church and instead called themselves the Free Methodist Church. In 1847, they requested to join the new Wesleyan Methodist Connection, a denomination that preached the radical idea of immediate emancipation. This new denomination originated in Ohio. The same year, an intrepid, untested young minister arrived in Jamestown. Adam Crooks would lead the new battle against enslavement in the North Carolina Piedmont.[137]

Quakers in the Piedmont, while not as immediatist as Crooks and certainly not as vocal, allowed the new preacher to hold services in their buildings. Soon Crooks had organized eight congregations. The first actual Wesleyan Church building was constructed a mile south of Cane Creek Meeting in Snow Camp in late 1847 and into early 1848.

Led by the inspiring and, apparently, incendiary, Adam Crooks, the first Wesleyan Methodist churches in the South were gaining traction, including the one organized in Snow Camp in 1847, Freedom's Hill Wesleyan Church. Another congregation was organized west of Snow Camp in Quaker-heavy Randolph County in 1850. It should come as no surprise that this antislavery denomination quickly took root in the heart of the Quaker Belt. Indeed, Randolph County, according to L. McKay Whatley, was at the heart of abolitionism just before the Civil War. William Auman notes that as North Carolina Quakers gave up their fight against enslavement and moved west, the Wesleyans filled the antislavery void. Surprisingly, Wesleyan Church historian Bob Black notes that the fledgling Freedom's Hill congregation was composed of not only Methodists but also Quakers. And this presents a question: Why didn't those Quakers who disagreed with enslavement in this area just go to Cane Creek Meeting or even Spring Friends Meeting, just a few miles east?[138]

Bob Black has the answer. "Although Quakers were antislavery, many were gradualists because they feared abolitionism would lead to social upheaval and even war." Quakers are known for their conservative lifestyles, and the abolitionist movement in America was gaining a reputation as disruptive, even militant, and therefore a threat to society. The majority of Cane Creek Meeting wanted no part of such radical behavior, but clearly a few within the fold were disappointed in what they perceived as a lack of total conviction evidenced in immediate abolition. Thus, these Quaker malcontents reached out to the fledgling Wesleyan denomination.[139]

Within this Quaker community we see divisions. Members of Cane Creek Meeting overall were gradualists, while some Quakers in the small Snow Camp community assumed a stronger, more defiant and immediatist stance against enslavement. This double consciousness permeated every Quaker meeting in North Carolina. Perhaps the gradualists were simply more concerned about the safety of their members. Proslavery locals shot at Freedom's Hill Church, and the bullet holes are still in the original structure, which can be seen today on the campus of Southern Wesleyan University in Central, South Carolina. Aggression was a major part of this tension. Pastor Adam Crooks was violently dragged from the church and had to flee for his life. Indeed, in an August 2, 1851 article in the *Greensboro Patriot*, we read that a local committee met concerning Adam Crooks. They put a bounty on his head in hopes of removing him from the state. The article notes that Crooks was connected with the URR and antislavery societies that "steal negroes." The church temporarily abandoned its abolitionist bent, but in the 1850s, former Quaker Daniel Worth, "a fiery abolitionist from Indiana," who was reared in Centre Meeting in Guilford County, returned and virulently chastised laconic, gradualist Quakers. In an 1858 letter to his sister, he noted that a few Friends in the Cane Creek area were "excellent," which meant they met his high standards for immediate abolition. Some of these Quakers even attended his church.[140]

Still, in the story of Freedom's Hill Church, we see two things of importance. First, people in the Piedmont were sensitive about enslavement, to the point of violence even against their pacifist Quaker neighbors. Second, we see yet another way that some Quakers cooperated with others of different beliefs to aid runaways in their escape to freedom.

Quakers continued to fight among themselves over the issue of aiding and harboring slaves in the clandestine—not to mention, illegal—movement of fugitives to the North. Concerned that Quakers were more and more crossing legal and, oddly enough, moral lines and thus drawing inadvertent attention to other Friends and angering enslaving neighbors, the North Carolina Yearly Meeting declared in 1843, "We have therefore thought…to make known our long-established practice and utter disapproval of such interference in any way whatever." This did not stop some resolute Quakers, as an 1844 letter from Nathan Hill of New Garden Meeting reveals. He argued that URR participants generated ill will in Guilford County between Quakers and their neighbors. While noting that Quakers were "remiss and come far short of our duty in many respects," he goes on to explain that Quakers true to their heritage were not "prepared to plunge headlong into difficulties uncalled for and to pursue a fanatical course…contrary to the principles and practices inculcated by the founders of our society."[141]

Once again, we see that strict adherence to Quaker polity and beliefs overruled any conscientious disapproval of enslavement. Quakers were indeed against the Quakers who were against Quakers. Thus it seemed that the only way to truly attack enslavement was for some daring, conscientious Friends to step outside the solid norms of the Society of Friends.

QUAKERS VERSUS NORTH CAROLINA

The conduct of the said Quakers in setting their slaves free when our open and declared enemies were endeavoring to bring about an insurrection of the Slaves, was highly criminal and reprehensible.
—Joint Committee of the North Carolina legislature (January 26, 1779), in Dungy, "A Friend in Deed," 19

Quakers in North Carolina were up against quite a legal and cultural wall if they were moved by their consciences to free both their enslaved and their unease. When Thomas Newby requested advice from the Perquimans Monthly Meeting on how to free his bondspeople in 1774, the matter was referred to the North Carolina Yearly Meeting. The Yearly Meeting decided that Quakers should approach their own meetings and these meetings would then arrange for appropriate members to draw up manumission papers if it was determined that the freed enslaved could provide for themselves. The local meeting also would determine if a Friend could purchase or sell an enslaved person. The meetings were also to devise plans to protect the freed enslaved people from capture. The Yearly Meeting even provided much-needed legal help for those wishing to manumit. It was needed because some of their members were breaking the law.[142]

With these guidelines in place, in 1777, Newby and nine other Quaker enslavers in the Perquimans area defied the 1741 law that forbade manumitting their enslaved except for "meritorious" services. Ironically, some of the enslaved, fearful of their freedom, potential recapture, and consequent sale back into servitude, came back to Newby and begged to be "bound for life" in exchange for protection. In essence, the freed person became enslaved to the Quaker again.[143]

This action was not allowed by the Quaker establishment. But it did provide a precedent that would lead to what Quakers in North Carolina would call "Free Negroes." What followed was a game of tit for tat between the North Carolina Quakers and the Colony and then the State of North Carolina.

Before 1741, an enslaved person could be manumitted for any reason by anyone in North Carolina without any court action or document. However, as the enslaved population increased, so did racial fears. Legislators responded by enacting a law in 1741 that allowed for manumission only for "meritorious services." Additionally, manumissions had to be approved by the courts and the freed enslaved had to leave the colony in six months or face capture and re-enslavement.

What exactly was meant by "meritorious services" and *who* determined the parameters? Some examples were saving a master from drowning or from a farm accident or simply providing years of faithful service. The court was not clear or even consistent on this matter; in some instances, it declared infants free based on "meritorious services."[144]

Quakers in Perquimans County used the meritorious services argument to help Peter, a "Servant Man" of Indian and Black descent. He was manumitted by Samuel Smith, and while he had not been captured to be enslaved again, local Quakers wished to ensure he remained free. Thus, they petitioned the county court on his behalf. Peter, they claimed, had never violated the law and in fact had protected locals by "Destroying Vermin Such as Bears Wolves wild Cats and Foxes."[145]

As we have seen, by the mid-1700s and especially into the Revolutionary years, some Quakers had begun listening to their conscience as well as the Declaration of Independence and looked for ways within the Quaker discipline to manumit their enslaved. But the enslaved were not leaving the state as required by law. Instead, they remained in the care and protection of the Quakers who manumitted them.

Quakers debated manumission during the time of the American Revolution. There was much talk of human rights, freedom, liberty, and equality. Would the enslaved of non-Quakers see the freeing of their fellow bondspeople as an incentive to demand their own freedom? If other enslaved people were indeed freed, would they be enticed to join the ranks of the British and take revenge on their former owners? Along with this, the fear of slave revolts was always in the minds of the whites, but it was especially heightened during the Revolutionary War as the British invited enslaved people to defect from their masters and fight against them.

Thus, as if to emphasize a point, the legislature passed another law in 1775 forbidding manumitting enslaved people if not approved by the courts. In 1777, the legislature reaffirmed the 1741 law with the further stipulation that any enslaved person manumitted illegally was to be captured immediately, jailed, and then sold back into enslavement at the next court session. Scholar Katherine Dungy concludes, "This could be seen as a direct response to the Quaker manumission movement."[146]

After the bill was passed, the Quakers reassessed their actions. It was discovered that all their enslaved manumitted by that time in Perquimans and Pasquotank sadly had been captured and re-enslaved without any court proceedings. Clearly, a new plan was needed. The Friends believed that the capture and sale of newly freed people released before 1777 violated the law, but their arguments met with a legislative wall. As North Carolina Friends continued to release their enslaved and thus leave them to fend for themselves, the legislature fought back.

In 1778, a new law was passed that allowed citizens to report illegally freed bondspeople and receive a reward as well. The court could immediately seize anyone freed from enslavement. This was especially ironic (or fortuitous?) given that many local courts were increasingly lax in their enforcement of the meritorious service clause. Indeed, the courts were often picking up the ones they had once freed and now selling them back to enslavers. When the law was initiated in January 1779, it was clear that it was in reaction to the Quakers. While part of this law made it illegal to capture a freed person and take him/her out of state, Quakers fought back with a petition that echoed language from the Declaration of Independence as well as their faith. It was signed by the same men who freed their enslaved in 1777. And beginning in 1779, persistent Quakers from Perquimans and Pasquotank flooded the courts with requests to free their enslaved. At the same time, the courts sent out summons to Quakers who had illegally released their enslaved people. This back-and-forth lasted into the early nineteenth century.

In 1785, a bill to allow conscientious objectors to enslavement to free their enslaved failed to pass. A 1786 law stipulated that freed slaves brought into North Carolina had to leave in three months. Free Blacks were denied travel on ships in 1787. This was no doubt to stymie the increasing use of the MRR to northern freedom. In 1788, the release of the enslaved based on religious principles was deemed dangerous. The hiring out of enslaved people who lived and worked as if free was declared illegal as of 1794. In 1795, free Blacks entering the state as well as Black people who were freed from that year forward had to pay a $200 bond. A $100 bond had to be paid for each enslaved released.[147]

Defiant eastern North Carolina Quakers ignored the laws and released their enslaved, who were then haplessly caught in the middle of conscientious Quakers and the ever-frustrated North Carolina legislators.

Within this legal maelstrom, freed Blacks sought out Friends to help them fight the system.

Former enslaved people freed by Quaker owners were often "taken up" by slave traders, sheriffs, and even local citizens and then sold back into servitude, as was the case with Thomas Pool's enslaved man Job. Job apparently had escaped this second bondage and had found asylum among sympathetic Quakers. Since there was a maritime "railroad" in existence at this time in Hampton Roads, Virginia, we can assume that, with Quakers in the Perquimans area, there could have been such a means of escape by sea to the North as well. Still, seeing all people as equal children of God meant manumission *but* taking care of one's neighbor might necessitate holding them in some kind of servitude to prevent them from being resold into a more oppressive household or plantation. Each action risked imprisonment for the conscientious Quaker.

Was it fair to release bondspeople if they had no real chance of success in their new life of freedom? The North Carolina Yearly Meeting realized that most enslaved had no real skills, few if any owned land, and nearly all had no tools with which to toil and earn an income. North Carolina ex-enslaved Harriet Jacobs, sometimes critical of her own race, points out that many slaves did not "understand their own capabilities" and thus they would not "exert themselves to become men and women." Further, such "inferiority" came about by the "ignorance in which the white men compel [the slave] to live." Her answer to this was for the slave to be "partially civilized" (educated) and "Christianized." This was the very same argument that Quakers had asserted in years past beginning with founder George Fox: Educate the enslaved so that they might be successful on release. Thus empowered, the former bondswoman or man would have the skills to take on the enslavement institution and even escape, survive, and become successful.[148]

There were other considerations as well. Jacobs observes that after the Nat Turner Slave Revolt in 1831, there was a marked shift in thinking. The fear of the enslaved gathering by themselves to ostensibly plan another revolt led enslavers to ban their chattel from gathering in small groups or even attending their own private Sunday services. Instead, they were now required to attend the white churches where the white preachers inculcated the biblical teachings that justified their servitude. As Jacobs concludes, "Slaveholders came to the conclusion that it would be well to give slaves enough of religious instruction to keep them from murdering their masters." Were Quakers considering the welfare of their neighbors if they freed those who might foment a rebellion?[149]

There was one answer awaiting them.

QUAKER FREE NEGROES

Let me give you a little account of our visit to the Slaveholders...of 12th month at the house of G.M. [George Mendenhall] *Slaveholder....I think there are six belonging to the house....The rest are hired out. There are one hundred in all. Delphina, his wife, is entirely opposed to slavery....The number I saw there are treated well, as slaves, yet 'tis as slaves. They are deprived of Liberty and the sin of the dreadful system remains the same.*
—Harriet Peck (1838), in a letter, in Browning, "Harriet Peck at New Garden Boarding School," 21

The confusing, often convoluted, and divisive nature of slavery among Quakers can be best summarized by the troubles and tensions within the Quaker Mendenhall family centered in Jamestown. Devoted Quaker George C. Mendenhall was disowned by Deep River Meeting when he married non-Quaker Eliza Dunn, an enslaver. George, a wealthy landowner and businessman, served in the Meeting for Sufferings and employed a progressive style of chattel productivity, in essence an industrial labor farm. George refused to sell his enslaved, but for good reason: he wished to keep enslaved families together and protect his enslaved from the harsh persecutions of enslavement in the Deep South, practiced by many empathetic enslavers as recalled by former North Carolina slaves. He also bought fugitives who fled to him seeking asylum from harsh masters. His enslaved population rose so that he was possibly the largest enslaver in Guilford County. But his enslaved had to be fed, clothed, and housed. Thus, he made sure they learned a trade. Some were clerks in his stores, both in sales and acquisitions, and some supervised his shops. Many were hired out to other farmers in the area.[150]

After the death of Eliza, George married antislavery advocate Delphina Gardner. Local lore recalls that Delphina helped Quaker David Beard, a hatter, hide fugitives on the run, often under pelts to be used for hats. Beard was an abolitionist and was known as the local URR head. Together George and Delphina planned how to free their enslaved. Beginning in 1835, they worked within the legal restraints of North Carolina laws to remove their bondspeople to Ohio. The process was tediously long and was not finished when George died in 1859. George's death meant that Delphina was now an enslaver. She honored George's wishes and began the slow removal of her enslaved overland to free states.[151]

The process of manumission was interrupted by her stepson James Ruffin Mendenhall, who contended his father's will. The North Carolina Supreme Court ruled in favor of George's wish that his enslaved, under the direction of his wife, Delphina, be freed. Hidden within this story is yet another step toward manumission and abolition: "free Negroes," who, though in some sense, were still enslaved, worked and lived as if independent. And these "free Negroes" were slowly taken from the enslaving South to the free Northwest by Quakers.[152]

By 1775, the North Carolina Yearly Meeting insisted that all Quakers release their bondspeople. This move in itself would result in substantial economic losses: the loss of money paid for the slaves, posting bonds for security, funding their mandated exit from the state. The cost of removing sixty-three freed bondsmen and women in 1826 was $1,093.81 for the Yearly Meeting. The meeting set up a committee to advise and assist members as they followed suit. Forty enslaved walked away from servitude the following year, but in 1777, the North Carolina General Assembly enacted a law quite similar to that of 1741 and soon sheriffs were rounding up the newly freed and selling them back into bondage, most likely in fear that they would organize an insurrection. Quakers protested this new law, but their words were ignored by the legislature. Friends responded in one of two ways. Some defied the law and still freed their enslaved, but this defiance came at a risk: The freed person could easily be caught and sold by unscrupulous slavecatchers. Hilty describes a cycle, as evidenced in a previous chapter, where northeastern North Carolina Quakers would then purchase these jailed freed people who were then freed once more. Others, afraid of this very result, thought it best to retain their enslaved but allowed them to work in freedom, which was just another form of enslavement.[153]

The story of Benjamin Stanton of Core Sound Meeting demonstrates further issues conscientious Quakers had to confront. He released the enslaved he inherited from his father in 1787. Benjamin and his widow and children protected them from capture, which would have required at the very least feeding them. Still, the family took some of these enslaved to Ohio (others may have elected to stay in the area, possibly due to family living nearby) when they migrated there in 1800.[154]

Quakers, frustrated and tired of the legal manipulations of the North Carolina judicial and political system, looked for legal help, and in 1808–9 they found it in the person of jurist William Gaston, who was emerging in the Tarheel State as a promising lawyer. He pursued human rights through the dictates of the Constitution.

Gaston doggedly searched for a legal precedent allowing Quakers to release their enslaved without fear of retribution from the state or from neighbors. He located an act from 1796 in which the North Carolina General Assembly approved a bill allowing the trustees of religious bodies to accept gifts. In this act was a clause reading, "Donations of personal property, such as money, slaves etc., may be receiv'd to any amount." This opened the door for the Friends of North Carolina to manumit their enslaved in a different way. Now Friends' chattel could be given to the trustees of the Yearly Meeting. Reaction was not swift, but Friends, wary of potential legal issues, hesitantly agreed to accept these "freed Negroes" (thus, ironically, still participating in the slave trade), and by 1814, 350 formerly enslaved Blacks were under the care of the Yearly Meeting, the number rising to 729 by 1826.[155]

In the Digital Library on American Slavery, there are ten thousand documents covering thirteen North Carolina counties concerning the transactions of enslavers. Those that mention Quakers all stem from the early to mid-1800s. All follow a standard format, suggesting that meetings were sent a sample template to be filled in by the grantor: "I [name] of the county and state aforesaid, for and in consideration of for the love and affection I have and do bear toward the Society of Friends, or people called Quakers." Based on these documents, several trends appear. First, there were two centers of "free Negroes," Perquimans Friends in the northeastern section of North Carolina and Centre Friends in the

Guilford County area in the Piedmont. Second, expectedly, the most slaves released were near the coast. Third, some enslavers actually lived in Ohio and Indiana, part of an exodus of Quakers from the slave culture of North Carolina. While some Friends migrated to the Northwest to avoid the slave culture altogether, they inexplicably, uncharacteristically, left their enslaved in North Carolina. In 1826 alone, ninety-five slaves were left behind by Friends. Perhaps these slaves wanted to remain near "home," where family lived. Still, without supervision, they were at risk: they could be sold.[156]

In the northeastern portion of the state, beginning in 1809, Friends in Perquimans were deeded fifteen enslaved from Thomas White. From 1809 to 1832 Perquimans Meeting received the deeds of over two hundred Blacks. While many families only enslaved two or three people, some released as many as fourteen. Rich Square Meeting saw similar results. John Peele transferred his sixty enslaved to his sons Edmund and Thomas, who then transferred them over to the trustees of the meeting in 1809. Edmund also owned fourteen enslaved people through his wife who were transferred to the meeting. Along with this, twenty were sent to Indiana, twenty-eight to Liberia in 1827, and another fifty-eight "who doubtless were also sent to Liberia."[157]

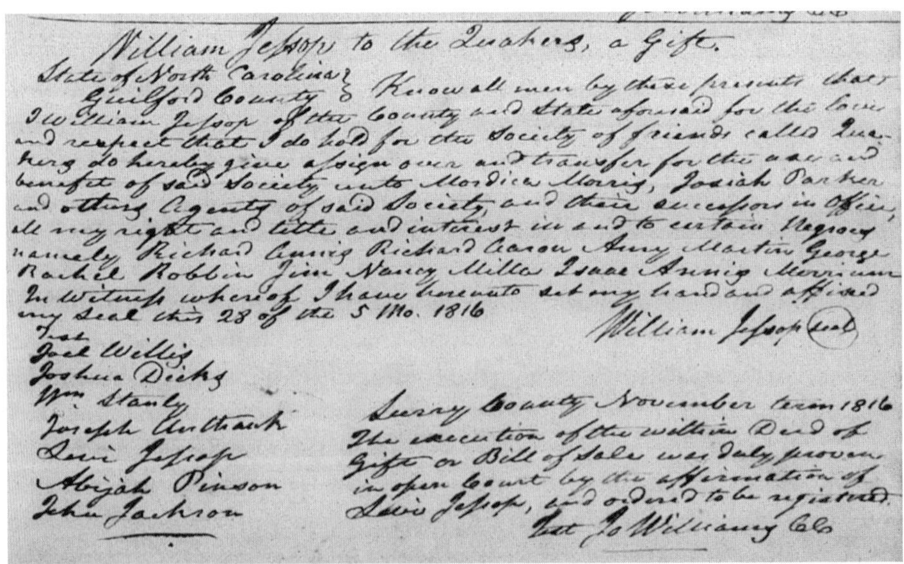

William Jessop to the Quakers, a Gift.

State of North Carolina } Guilford County } Know all men by these presents that I William Jessop of the County and State aforesaid for the love and respect that I do hold for the Society of Friends called Quakers do hereby give assign over and transfer for the use and benefit of said Society unto Mordica Morris, Josiah Parker and others, Agents of said Society, and their successors in Office, all my right and title and interest in and to certain Negroes namely Richard Annis Richard Aaron Amy Martin George Rachel Robbin Jim Nancy Milla Isaac Annis Morrison In Witness whereof I have hereunto set my hand and affixed my seal this 28 of the 5 Mo. 1816

William Jessop (seal)

Test
Joel Willis
Joshua Dicks
Wm. Stanly
Joseph Arthur [illegible]
Levi Jessop
Abijah Pinson
John Jackson

Surry County November term 1816
The execution of the within Deed of Gift or Bill of Sale was duly proven in open Court by the affirmation of Levi Jessop, and ordered to be registered.
Test Jo Williams Clo

The 1816 deed of William Jessop releasing his enslaved to the Society of Friends. *Digital Library on American Slavery*.

In 1815 and 1816, in the Piedmont, Centre Friends Meeting in Guilford County was deeded several unnamed bondspeople by four different enslavers: Nathan Pearson of Indiana released "all the Negroes and Mulattows [*sic*] and children thereof belonging to the estate of Isaac Lamb"; Josiah Lamb and David Bailey, both of Indiana; and Isaac Brown of Randolph County, North Carolina. Their enslaved were deeded over to "Robert McCrackon, Joe Worth, Peter Dicks, Dugan Clark, Zeno Worth and David Worth as Trustees and agents Acting in Trust for the Monthly Meeting of Friends Commonly Called Quakers." In May 1816, William Jessup of Surry County, "for the love and respect that I do hold for the Society of Friends," released to the Quakers of Guilford County fifteen bondspeople. In the same month, he released another fourteen. That year, Ann Benbow of Guilford County also released her seven enslaved to Mordecai Morris and Josiah Parker "and other agents" of the Society.[158]

In 1818, Lewis Hornaday of Orange County deeded his eight enslaved to trustees Solomon Dixon, Hugh Woody, and Joseph Hill of Orange County. Thomas Carter, Archibald Edwards, and Nathaniel Edwards, all of Ohio, deeded their bondspeople to the Trustees Nathaniel Newlin and Thomas Newlin of Orange County, North Carolina, in 1819. The next year, again we see Solomon Dixon, Hugh Woody, and Joseph Hill of Orange and Chatham Counties, North Carolina—now listed as North Carolina Yearly Meeting trustees—received a deed for John Long's enslaved. These men were part of the Cane Creek and Spring Friends Meetings.[159]

In 1816, William Jessup of Westfield Friends Meeting gave his fifteen bondspeople over to the care of Mordecai Morris, Josiah Parker, and other agents of the Society of Friends. While William's conscience was piqued enough to follow through on this good deed, this benevolent spirit did not run through his family. His two brothers did not follow suit.[160]

While the intent of the Quakers was admirable, the ownership of these "free Negroes" brought immediate problems. The North Carolina Yearly Meeting trustees individually took in and cared for the bondspeople, but how would the Quakers fund the needs of these former enslaved? Housing, clothes, and food were needed. Male bondsmen were hired out to local businessmen and received wages, part of which were retained by the trustees to care for women, children, the elderly, and those with handicaps. But should they be hired out to Friends who were "insensitive"—that is, who were not opposed to enslavement? Along with this, Friends trustees in the eastern portion of North Carolina cried foul since they had a disproportionate number to support compared to trustees in the Piedmont. What about North Carolina Quaker trustees who set out for Ohio and Indiana, leaving their wards to fend for themselves? Recall that Rich Square Meeting in Northampton County may have had as many as three hundred "free Negroes" under their care. Who would assume the care of these former enslaved? And why would "sensitive" trustees leave the "free Negroes" under their care anyway? Why not take them along on the journey north?[161]

There were legal issues as well. For a century, the North Carolina Friends were involved in numerous lawsuits. Heirs of deceased Friends, such as Jacob White, who transferred his bondspeople over to his meeting, demanded they be returned to the family. In another case, the issues were quite complicated. John Newlin of Spring Friends Meeting, a member of the North Carolina Manumission Society and a Quaker lobbyist to the North Carolina General Assembly, was deeded around forty Black enslaved (the sources disagree on the number) by neighbor Sarah Freeman, who was not a Quaker. She knew of the Quaker Free Negro program and knew that Newlin would help free her enslaved people. Two problems arose. First, because it took months, even years to arrange for the proper removal of freed slaves, Newlin was stuck "owning" former enslaved people. In order to feed, clothe, and house them in the interim, he "hired" them to work on his millrace. In the eyes of many, this was participating in the enslavement institution. To make matters worse, the Freeman family contested the will, and it took ten years to resolve. What was Newlin to do? Eventually, after a decade, he was able to carry out the wishes of Sarah Freeman.[162]

The North Carolina Courts also questioned the legitimacy of this Quaker "subterfuge" of deeding enslaved persons over to the meeting. The court increasingly ruled against the practice when its legality was questioned. In 1817, one man was given to the trustees of Contentnea Meeting by William Dickinson, "to be kept at work but to receive the profits of his labor, and ultimately to be free when his freedom could be effected by the laws of the state." Unfortunately, by North Carolina law, any freed slave must leave the state within ninety days of manumission. This Quaker practice risked violation of the law, and Quakers, by rule, were averse to breaking any laws of the state.

Since it was now against Quaker belief to enslave anyone, Quaker trustees of the Yearly Meeting harboring "free Negroes" was still considered enslavement. Undaunted, Quakers took the odd, ironic, and apparently illegal route of the Yearly Meeting, holding the formerly enslaved until freedom could be negotiated.[163]

Once Quakers emancipated their own bondspeople, another question arose: How would/did North Carolina Quakers incorporate Blacks, enslaved and free, into their society and religion? Fox and Woolman insisted on educating slaves. If invited to join the sect, then training, both social and religious, could lead to a stronger society and more empowered people. As part of the industrious Quaker community, new skills could be taught, life lessons shared, cultural norms instilled. Unfortunately, the efforts were not entirely successful. Some Quakers, however, doggedly persevered. George Walton of Perquimans noted in his journal that a "Meeting for the Blacks" was organized in 1777 at Piney Woods. Whether this was for freed Blacks or their enslaved is not clear. After "many good Counsels & Exhortation[s]," he felt the Blacks were "tender" and that they would remember the "good Advice given them." He also said this about meetings with white Quakers.[164]

In the Piedmont, New Garden Friends expressed a desire to incorporate Blacks into their meetings in 1798. The matter was considered by a committee in the Yearly Meeting, but after two years, the Yearly Meeting denied the request. Quaker historian Hiram Hilty concludes that "North Carolina Friends as a whole were far too conservative to approve such an adventurous move at that time."[165]

According to Aptheker, in general, the Quaker plan to integrate free Blacks into their religious society "is far from inspiring." He cites evidence that Quakers overall, if they were inclined to have Blacks in their services, required them to sit in what he called "Jim Crow sections" and what was often referred to as the "Negro Pew." This was indeed the case in at least one Quaker meeting. When Cane Creek Meeting rebuilt their meetinghouse after a fire destroyed the previous structure, "The gallery for the freed slaves [was] not replaced in the new building." This statement must be true because Cane Creek Friend Solomon Allen's household included freed slaves. Aptheker concludes that evidence demonstrates that, for North Carolina Friends, a "Negro Quaker was highly exceptional."[166]

If Quakers were indeed reluctant to invite their enslaved into their meetings, there was another way to incorporate them into the industrious

Free Black people lived in small enclaves on farms in the Piedmont area. This structure is near Centre Meeting, just on the Guilford/Randolph County line. The building was enlarged and is now used for storage on a local farm. *By the author.*

Quaker society. Robert Pleasants, a Virginia Quaker, followed the model of the indentured servant when he set aside some of his lands and offered his support for them for one year, presumably so that they could learn the necessary skills and acquire enough funds to move forward on their own. Indeed, in North Carolina "free Negroes" were placed on "test farms" to see if they were skilled enough to live and succeed on their own. North Carolina Friends were finding ways to both circumvent the system and empower freed Blacks.[167]

The Peter Newby family, who lived near Centre Meeting but were not Quakers, enslaved several Black people, and local Quakers helped free them sometime before 1800. This included bondsmen George and Moses. William Dennis, a member of Centre Meeting and later clerk for Marlboro Meeting, took George under his wing as an apprentice just as any other Quaker would have trained his own child. According to records, George was to be educated in ways that would ensure a successful life of freedom. Moses, who was born some twenty years prior to George, apprenticed as a potter to John Bullock of Orange County in 1798. In the legal ruling, it was determined that Moses was of good moral character and was now a master of a trade. With this, he was allowed to continue as a free man.[168]

While these efforts were quite altruistic, they were also required by a 1762 North Carolina law. Children of free Blacks were to be bound out as apprentices until the age of twenty-one. In this time, the child was to be taught a trade and clothed, fed, and taught to read and write. The law also extended to Black children whose free parents could not properly care for them. The law was further extended in 1826 to children whose parents were not employed in an "honest and industrious occupation." In 1838, the law was changed, now prohibiting teaching reading and writing.[169]

We see here that "freedom" came for some as an indenture or an apprenticeship to learn a trade that would be fruitful and lead to a life of financial independence. Freedom also was acquired as Quakers like Vestal Coffin of Guilford County sold land to freed Blacks, thus allowing them to farm and earn a living. Other freed Blacks were allowed to live on land owned by whites. Most were independent farmers, and some, like Ellis Mitchell, who was also a blacksmith, fared quite well. One unforeseen effect, however, was that freed Blacks could offer asylum to runaways, and this would explain why many fugitives aimed for Guilford and Randolph Counties.[170]

However, what was supposed to be a benevolent, temporary solution to a never-ending problem became something of a pariah. The growing problem was no doubt racial. The freed Black population in Guilford County rose considerably between 1820 and 1840, outpacing the white population. Given the fears of revolts by Blacks, free and enslaved, and the possible negative influence of freed Blacks on those still in bondage, it was certain that whites would worry over this increase. Along with this, it was now easier for fugitives to hide among freed Blacks. Since most Quakers were not inclined to take part in the social, legal, and political dangers of manumission and abolition, we can surmise that many Quakers also feared this increase taking place in their own backyards.[171]

The URR began in an effort to deal with the frustrating problems that freed Blacks, not runaways, presented to the Quakers. With this increasing Black population in the Piedmont, the role of Blacks in what would eventually be called the URR increased. Free Blacks lent their manumission papers to fugitives, claiming they were stolen. Fugitives then carried them while being escorted by migrating Quakers on their journey north. Addison Coffin describes a similar process as part of the URR. Arch Curry, a free Black man living near Coffin's home in New Garden, Guilford County, died, leaving a widow, Vina, who worked as a washerwoman at what is now Guilford College. Freed Blacks had to carry their papers with them at all times. Now that Arch was gone, his papers could be put to good use. When a likely fugitive arrived in the New Garden area, as happened quite often, who fit her husband's description and there was a family heading northwest, she lent her husband's free papers to him. Levi Coffin, then living in Indiana, would bring the papers back, and the ruse was continued over the years for a total of fifteen times.[172]

At the request of the Friends in the Deep River Quarter, the North Carolina Yearly Meeting investigated the feasibility of moving their enslaved to the Midwest. One major question to answer was if there were any laws that would prevent such a plan. After a year's deliberation, this request was granted, and in 1823, nine "slaves" of the North Carolina Yearly Meeting left the home of their servitude; eight headed for Indiana, the other for Philadelphia.[173]

The following year, twenty-four enslaved people divided into two groups left for the Midwest. In 1825, two more groups were taken to their freedom in the Midwest. The journey was not without hazards, however, as Levi Coffin recalls throughout his *Reminiscences*. Bandits, slave catchers, and bounty hunters haunted the roads looking to steal any Black person they could find. What does a pacifist Quaker say to such brigands who wielded guns, clubs, and whips? Should resistance be offered? In one instance, a Friend had to purchase back a former slave who was apprehended. In another, a Black man was stolen, but a year later he was discovered by persistent Quakers and brought to freedom.[174]

As Friends began this program, the president of Haiti, Jean-Pierre Boyer, revealed an enticing incentive to Blacks, free and enslaved. Incessant wars on the island led to loss of labor on the sugar plantations. Upon arrival in Haiti, the freedmen and women would receive land, tools, and the necessary provisions for one year so that these new farmers could settle down with some ease. Others were to work on the sugar plantations. North Carolina Friends, as did the North Carolina Manumission Society, whose president, Aaron Coffin, heartily endorsed the plan, saw only vast opportunities for Black people in Haiti. A choice was offered: Haiti would cover expenses of those who chose to wander about uncultivated lands and settle down; others could purchase already improved lands, or they could become tenants or sharecroppers.

As Blacks in northeastern America took advantage of this offer—between six and seven hundred left for a new life on the island—North Carolina Quakers, always cautious, deliberated over the plan. In the meantime, they set up a Meeting for Sufferings (a committee, not an actual meeting place for worship), which then allowed trustees to hire out their wards and use the wages to cover their debts and set aside funds to help in their removal to other places such as Haiti and the Midwest.[175]

The Meeting for Sufferings needed funds for the removal of enslaved and free Blacks, and Quakers responded in kind. In 1826, 120 Blacks were sent to Haiti, 316 to Liberia, and 110 to Ohio and Indiana. Prior to this, 11 were taken to Africa, 47 to Liberia, and 64 to Ohio. Each batch of Black emigrants required enormous sums of money for the journey. In 1827, the Meeting for Sufferings reported receiving $3,000 from the Philadelphia Yearly Meeting, $1,000 from Rhode Island, and $1,100 from London Yearly Meeting, as well as other substantial funds from meetings far and wide. This supported the removal of 543 Blacks in 1828, but with 501 more waiting, more funds were needed.[176]

While an intriguing and no doubt altruistic vision, what was the difference in this new plan and the common practice of hiring out other enslaved to plantation owners whereby the enslaver would receive the wages earned? Ex-enslaved Solomon Northup asked this very question. In some instances, the bondsperson was allowed to keep a portion of the wages, and sometimes he or she would offer to work in such a capacity for other owners on his or her day off and was thus allowed to keep the extra wages. If the enslaved were indeed "free" in everything but name, why weren't they given the full wages and then left to pay their own debts and their way to freedom? Were the enslaved still seen as untrustworthy, incapable of taking care of themselves?[177]

Taking up the offer of land grants and other incentives from Haiti, in 1824, North Carolina Friends Meeting for Sufferings initiated the drive to send Blacks there. By 1825, Eastern North Carolina Quakers had sent 506 people to Haiti. In 1826, another expedition of 119 left from Beaufort on the *Sally Ann*, the first of several groups sent out on this ship. These included former enslaved from as far inland as Deep River Meeting in the Piedmont who were accompanied by Phineas Nixon and John Fellow. After a few years, however, the situation in Haiti turned sour. Conditions there became hostile for some, and Blacks felt pressured to settle there when they preferred to stay in North Carolina. In one instance, an enslaved person attacked his owner because he wanted to send him to the island against his will.[178]

The focus then turned to Liberia, a nation created on the west coast of Africa by the American Colonization Society as a new land. North Carolina Friends such as Isaac Overman, Jeremiah Hubbard, Richard and Nathan and Mary Mendenhall, Phineas Albertson, Caleb and Miles White, Jonas Mace, and George Swaim enthusiastically endorsed the plan. The notion was to send enslaved African Americans back to their "ancestral home." Ignoring the stories of ex-enslaved being recaptured there and then sold back into slavery, North Carolina Friends raised the extensive funds to ship freed slaves to their "homeland" from 1827 to 1831. Sailing from Norfolk, freed slaves who endured the arduous journey overland sailed on the *Doris*, the *Nautilus* and the *American* in successive trips to the "land of their forefathers." Josiah Parker of Rich Square Meeting in Eastern Quarter and a member of the Meeting for Sufferings and John Kennedy from Wayne County, along with Aaron White and his wife, were some of the Friends who assisted the travelers. Josiah took forty-one now-freed Blacks to Norfolk, where they boarded a ship for Liberia. The women of Eastern Quarterly Meeting made new clothes for them. It is possible that a Black Masons community was involved in these endeavors, as the one in Norfolk was known to be part of the URR. The drive for deportation continued, but it was fraught with potential disaster and there were some initial failures. Lester Craig Cannon Jr. recalls that Quakers from Carteret County bought ships and sailed from Beaufort "with hundreds of slaves" for Jamaica and Liberia. However, they were not happy there and wanted to return to Carteret County.[179]

Passages to Africa were perilous and uncomfortable for the hopeful. They could be stuffed together with cargo; there was often sickness and the usual danger of Atlantic storms. Prayer meetings were held along the way both to assuage fears and instill hope, and Friends who accompanied these formerly enslaved in their passage taught them the necessary mindsets to be successful in their new environs. Surprises, such as unexpected port fees, often awaited the Friends who escorted the wary Blacks. Migration *within* America continued as well; Henry Ballinger led forty former enslaved to Indiana, and John White escorted fifty-four to Ohio and Indiana.[180]

While some of these endeavors were successful, many were not. Northern states were closing their doors to runaways and free Blacks.

Failed colonies and harsh treatment in other lands were becoming the norm. These negative accounts soon reached the ears of Blacks who still belonged to the Yearly Meeting. Thus, resistance to the removal plans arose among those who were willing to risk living in North Carolina rather than hope that all went well in a foreign land or state. Still, between 1833 and 1835, North Carolina Quakers begged people of color to reconsider their decision to remain in the state.[181]

Whether the intentions of the Society were sincere has been questioned by some scholars. Comments within the Society's documents suggest many of its members, based on their observations of enslaved behavior and culture, believed all Blacks inferior to whites. Alexis de Tocqueville, in his astute observations of Americans, suggested that the main issue for the colonizationists was that white Americans simply did not want to mingle with freed Blacks. Many Quakers quietly agreed.[182]

Still, other Quakers persevered. There had to be a way to achieve physical freedom for the oppressed slave and spiritual release for the Quaker of conscience.

QUAKERS AND THE MEETING FOR SUFFERINGS

Your memorialists are emboldened under a weighty sense of religious duty to petition the present General Assembly to repeal all those laws...against the literary instruction of slaves....And they also respectfully request your consideration of the repeal of the laws recently enacted prohibiting all colored persons in this state...from preaching or exhorting publicly in their respective religious congregations.

—Memorial from the Meeting on Sufferings to the North Carolina General Assembly (1834), in A Narrative of Some of the Proceedings of the North Carolina Yearly Meeting on the Subject of Slavery Within Its Limits, *34*

Quakers, from their inception by George Fox, countered contemporary English social, political, and religious norms. Refusing to honor deference because all were equal, honoring the Light within rather the bishop of the Anglican Church, industrious to a fault yet bound to a life of simplicity, everything the Friends stood for threatened the social, political, and religious structures of the British Isles. The result of their preferred lifestyle was persecution and ostracization. Thus Quakers were quite familiar with hardship, and in 1675, they organized a Meeting for Sufferings.

The Meeting for Sufferings in London initially focused on the needs of the persecuted within their ranks. The first such meeting in the colonies was in Philadelphia, organized in 1759 to address the issues of the French and

Indian War. North Carolina Quakers followed suit in 1759. Only men served in the Meeting for Sufferings, and their focus eventually moved toward an executive committee overseeing Quaker matters.

As the colonies mustered for their war against their mother country, the North Carolina Meeting for Sufferings, acting more like a committee for doctrinal integrity, reminded North Carolina Quakers their pacifist teachings required resolute steadfastness against the "arbitrary injunctions and ordinances of men who assume to themselves the power of compelling others." Seen as traitors, North Carolina Friends were tormented by Loyalists and Patriots alike. In 1829, the meeting encouraged local meetings to develop plans to organize and acquire books for "a suitable library of books approved by the Society of Friends."[183]

As Quakers tackled the institution of enslavement in North Carolina, the Meeting for Sufferings administrated the efforts. As early as 1758, eastern North Carolina Quakers discussed the matter of organizing "Negro" meetings. In 1768, concerns arose over the buying and selling of Blacks was considered. Such matters were deliberated by the Standing Committee, which became the Meeting for Sufferings. Decades later, Richard Mendenhall was a key member of the meeting, and his service in the North Carolina legislature meant that politicians heard the voice of Quakers regarding enslavement. His brother George, a lawyer by trade, also worked within the meeting.[184]

In 1808, North Carolina Friends across the state began transferring their enslaved over to the Yearly Meeting. As numbers increased, so did the need for care and comfort, which came at considerable cost. Questions arose that the Meeting for Sufferings, which met in Jamestown, struggled to answer. Divisions escalated between Quakers as well. The issues for eastern Quakers, whose many enslaved toiled in mostly agricultural tasks, were more complex than those of Piedmont Quakers, whose few bondspeople were more domestic laborers. Quakers in eastern North Carolina wondered why more money was held in escrow for western freedmen and women when those funds could have been used to pay the expenses of the numerous freed Blacks down east. Overall, the management of the expenses to feed, house, and clothe the "Free Negroes," plus the additional funds needed for travel to the West, the islands, or Africa was tedious in itself. In 1826 alone, the ninety-five "Free Negroes" went to Ohio, fifty-

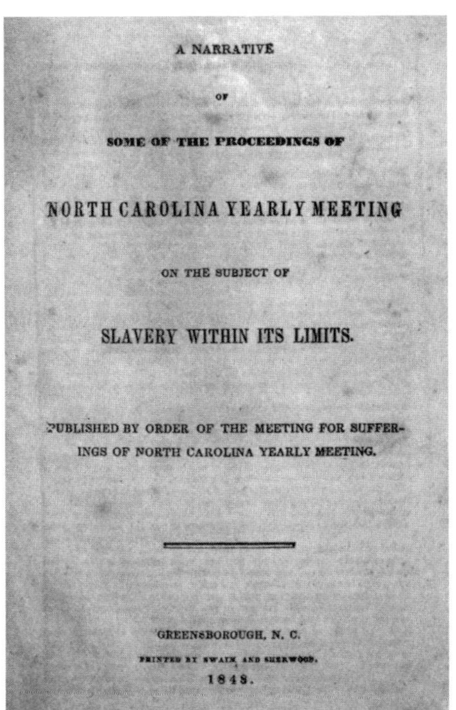
A NARRATIVE

OF

SOME OF THE PROCEEDINGS OF

NORTH CAROLINA YEARLY MEETING

ON THE SUBJECT OF

SLAVERY WITHIN ITS LIMITS.

PUBLISHED BY ORDER OF THE MEETING FOR SUFFERINGS OF NORTH CAROLINA YEARLY MEETING.

GREENSBOROUGH, N. C.

PRINTED BY SWAIM AND SHERWOOD.

1848.

In 1848, the North Carolina Yearly Meeting For Sufferings published a history of its actions concerning slavery and Blacks in general. *Public domain.*

eight to Liberia, and 119 to Haiti. That left 617 in the hands of the Yearly Meeting, 100 of which were caught up in legal battles of family wills and North Carolina laws. In the meantime, former chattel remained "enslaved" to the Yearly Meeting, and the Meeting for Sufferings had to manage their care, which consisted in hiring them out for service.[185]

Family squabbles over their bondspeople proved frustrating for the Meeting for Sufferings. Older Friends were more uneasy about enslavement than their children, who often contested their parents' wills. For example, Contentnea Quarterly Meeting in the Goldsboro area dealt with the Dickenson family. The father willed his sixteen bondsmen and women to the Yearly Meeting in 1817, yet his now non-Quaker children claimed six of them. Ten years later, the case came before Wayne County Superior Court. In the meantime, the enslaved in question had to be fed, housed, and hired out to cover their expenses. The Meeting for Sufferings oversaw this process.[186]

The same thing happened to John Newlin of Spring Meeting. As noted before, in 1839, non-Quaker Sarah Freeman bequeathed her thirty-nine (the sources differ on the number) slaves to him to be taken to freedom, but her children contested the will. For ten years, the matter was stalled in the courts. Meanwhile, Newlin, who spent much time with the Meeting for Sufferings, hired out these bondspeople to himself to work on and for his mill. The monies "earned" would help defray the $1,000 bond required for each emancipated person as stated by an 1830 law. Still, by law, freed enslaved people were required to leave the state in ninety days. In this sense, Newlin's ownership avoided legal punishment.[187]

The Meeting for Sufferings handled other cases as well, some lasting for years. In 1810, Quakers were sued by a free Black mother in Beaufort who wanted her two children released from Quaker ownership. It took three years to finalize the freedom of a free Black man, Benjamin Benson, who had been kidnapped and re-enslaved. In Carteret County, James Davis, a member of the Meeting for Sufferings, fought not only the court but also local abolitionists who feared what the emancipation of Mary might provoke. It took fifteen years to settle the case and free Quaker Thomas Wright's enslaved.[188]

The Quaker migrations westward to non-enslaving states was depleting the numbers of Quakers who could assist in these efforts. This placed even more responsibilities on the members of the Meeting for Sufferings. Tired of the meeting seemingly favoring the western Quakers, eastern Quakers generally took matters into their own hands, occasionally sending reports back to Jamestown. When North Carolina Quakers finalized their plan for "Free Negroes" in 1814, they restarted their Meeting for Sufferings in order to oversee and resolve the myriad problems that ensued with such a monumental decision. In 1825, the Eastern Quarterly Meeting notified the Meeting for Sufferings that they organized and sent a contingent to Haiti. In 1827, the Meeting for Sufferings allotted $1,132 for clothing for 142 passengers to Liberia.[189]

By 1848, Quakers had freed themselves from their slaves as well as their "unease" about slavery. It took nearly 100 years to fulfill John Woolman's vision of ending the Quaker enslavement to slavery. The Meeting for Sufferings submitted their final report to the Yearly Meeting. Their neighbors, however, still enslaved Blacks despite the efforts of the Friends. There was still more that needed to be done.

QUAKERS AND THE NORTH CAROLINA MANUMISSION SOCIETY

Slaves will go anywhere to be free.
—Moses Grandy (1843), in Andrews, North Carolina Slave Narratives, *183*

We are surrounded by Colonizationists though there are a few who go for immediate emancipation.
—Harriet Peck (1838), in Browning, "Harriet Peck," 17

I can testify, from my own painful experience, to the deep and fond affection which the slave cherishes in his heart for his home and its dear ones.
—Thomas Jones (1855; 1885), in Andrews, North Carolina Slave Narratives, *211*

I do not imagine that the white and black races will ever live in any country upon an equal footing.
—Alexis de Tocqueville (1835), Democracy in America, *433*

Quakers throughout the young nation were actively involved in the rise of manumission and eventually abolitionist societies. In most manumission societies, Quakers, generally wealthy merchants, were the majority members. Southern manumission societies were mostly ineffective and, predictably, preferred gradual manumission rather than instant abolition. Indeed, in many early societies founded in the late 1700s, it was believed that the enslaved who served "good masters" could be indoctrinated better into society than those who were instantly freed. In what might be termed a second wave of manumission society formation, the emphasis was more on ending enslavement and promotion of better treatment of freed slaves. In North Carolina, 80 percent of these societies were Quaker, and notably, most were founded by Friends who migrated from the North to the Tarheel State.[190]

The North Carolina Manumission Society, organized months before the American Colonization Society, first met at Centre Meeting in 1816. The names of these organizations reveal much about their intentions: manumission or colonization? The motivation for colonization was a divisive one. Questions and even fears arose for those concerned about enslavement, and underneath lay a latent prejudice. Once freed, what occupations were available? Would skilled Blacks take away jobs from whites? Where would freedmen and women live? What about miscegenation? Would former bondswomen and men rise up in arms against their enslavers? The fear, as Tocqueville observed, was that "the presence of a free negro vaguely agitates the mind of his less fortunate brethren." And beneath this fear was the ever-present worry of what Tocqueville, writing in the 1830s, presciently believed was an impending civil war between Blacks and whites. "The negroes…once raised to the level of free men, they will soon revolt at being deprived of all their civil rights." Early Quaker proponents of colonization had their doubts as to whether those of dark complexion, odd customs, and even different hair could mix with whites. Anthony Benezet suggested freed enslaved peoples be deported west to the new lands of America, even south to the newly purchased Louisiana Territory. Even Elijah Coffin proposed creating a new African nation somewhere in the wilderness of America. When the American Colonization Society acquired Liberia in Africa, the dilemma seemed solved. However, as altruistic whites paternalistically made plans for Blacks, the majority of Blacks in America preferred life in the states.[191]

Other questions arose. Colonization was for free Blacks; some Quakers such as Benjamin Lundy thought that the promotion of colonization might spur increased efforts toward emancipation. Semantics soon entered the discussion. What exactly did "colonization" mean? It seemed to imply a forced removal; the term "resettlement" was thus used to denote voluntary emigration. African American Quaker, whaling merchant, and abolitionist Paul Cuff argued for resettlement in Sierra Leon. Who would pay for this? Last, Southern politicians, especially in Guilford and Randolph Counties, saw the colonization society as a way to remove freed Blacks from their communities while retaining the institution of enslavement.[192]

Manumission societies in North Carolina were inspired by Quaker Charles Osborn, originally of Centre Meeting in southern Guilford County, right at the Randolph County border. He headed to Tennessee, which became a separate state from North Carolina in 1796, where he began to preach. He eventually visited all Southern Quaker meetings, where he addressed the issue of Quakers and enslavement. Years before William Lloyd Garrison began his antislavery crusade and before Quaker Benjamin Lundy published his first antislavery tract in 1821, Osborn proclaimed "the doctrine of immediate and unconditional emancipation." Osborn organized the Tennessee Manumission Society in 1814, and two years later he organized several societies in Guilford County. From there, he left for Ohio, where he published *The Philanthropist*, "the first journal in America to advocate unconditional emancipation."[193]

While Osborn attended to other manumission meetings and publications, two brothers, John and Robert Stuart, took over the reins of the new Tarheel Society. Nathan Hunt, from Springfield Friends Meeting, also assumed a leadership role. Other prominent Quakers included Jeremiah Hubbard; Richard, Nathan, and James Mendenhall; Aaron and Vestal Coffin; Asa Folger; Paul Macy and Paul Macy Jr.; Phineas Albertson; Daniel Worth; Phineas Nixon Jr.; Joseph Hunt; and John Beard. The North Carolina Manumission Society's rolls included an overwhelming number of Quakers, as manumission meetings were already being held in the Caraway community in Randolph County and at Centre, Deep River, and New Garden Meetings. As the general North Carolina Manumission Society formed, meetings were held alternately at Deep River and Centre Meetings.[194]

Nearly all of these early North Carolina Manumission Societies formed a line from the middle of Randolph County north into Guilford County, from Caraway community to New Garden Meeting. It is easy to postulate that this line of meetings, with its sympathies to the plight of the enslaved, would have been part of the URR as well. As we will see, one safe house was within a mile of Centre Meeting. By 1826, numerous societies convened in the Piedmont area, while only six met in the combined area of Goldsboro and the Albemarle region.

Other denominations were encouraged to join, but their initial enthusiasm distilled into nonattendance. By the fall of 1817, membership had increased to over 250, and this included 3 from the Coffin family: Levi, Vestal, and Elijah. The Society assessed the well-being of freed Blacks and worried over them being kidnapped and re-enslaved.

One little known part of this story is the involvement of Piedmont Quaker women. Women were not admitted to the North Carolina manumission societies, but that did not deter them from involvement in the cause. In 1825, nearly a decade before women in Philadelphia organized the Female Anti-Slavery Society, Guilford County Quaker women organized a female auxiliary to the manumission society meeting in Jamestown. Led by Elizabeth Mendenhall, women offered cloth, stockings, and their labor to sew items needed by the enslaved. Springfield Meeting and Centre Meeting soon organized auxiliaries as well. By 1830, forty-five female auxiliaries were offering their services to the cause.[195]

The North Carolina Manumission Society's work was hindered, however, by a division, and this story has an altruistic beginning. Enslavers around and south of Centre Meeting in Randolph County, aware of the Quakers' efforts to release their enslaved, oddly enough, were in favor of manumission *if* the freed Blacks were removed to Africa. There was already a large contingent of freed Blacks in the area due to the efforts of local Quakers following their conscience. In 1817, led by General Alexander Gray, a prominent enslaver in Randolph County, and supported by other enslavers, the North Carolina Manumission Society was encouraged to join the American Colonization Society. Enslavers wanted Blacks removed from the state, which meant colonization. Residents of Randolph and Guilford Counties agreed with the goals of gradual manumission and relocation by colonization.

General Gray was an astute, sensitive, and progressive farmer who understood the complexities of manumission versus colonization. One was simply economic. A $500 bond was required to release a slave, and if Gray released his eighty-three slaves in 1830, he would have lost nearly $42,000. Likewise, other enslavers and the North Carolina Yearly Meeting trustees faced overwhelming costs to free their Black wards. Along with this, a freed bondsperson had to leave the state in ninety days, which required more money, at least $200 per person. Even Quakers realized these economic pitfalls and, afraid of hurting their fellow neighbors in any way, stood against asking them to release their enslaved due to the economic losses that would be incurred. General Gray eventually ameliorated his stance to that of abolitionist and advocated that enslavers endeavor to teach their chattel the business of farming. This approach taught them skills to take care of themselves, including the basics of an education. It also kept them out of the bounty hunters' hands.[196]

Perhaps most important, it alleviated white fears of freed Blacks. In North Carolina, several revolts had been thwarted by whites. There is some question as to the veracity of these revolts since they were "reported" by local news and gossip. "Confessions" were attained after severe beatings, but tellingly, no revolt actually occurred in the Tarheel State, leading to speculation that rising fears among whites may have led to suspicions of revolts. One such "revolt" occurred in Beaufort County before the American Revolution. In 1802, "paroxysms of terror" spread through ten counties in the northeastern portion of the state over an insurrection planned for June 10. Residents, which included many Quakers, living near the Dismal Swamp, where runaways often fled and then settled down, were in constant danger of periodic guerrilla attacks by maroons, especially from 1775 to 1831.[197]

In 1805, a similar travesty took place in Wayne County, this time centered on poisoning whites. In 1831, shortly after the Nat Turner Revolt in Virginia, rumors of a similar revolt spread from Sampson County to the city of Raleigh and even farther west to Hillsborough. After militias were raised, arms and ammunition secured, it was revealed that one free man had concocted a plan for bondspeople in Duplin, Sampson, New Hanover, Lenoir, and Wayne Counties to march to Wilmington to raise arms and more recruits, none of which came to fruition. The son of the Sampson County sheriff admitted that innocent enslaved people were executed for no reason.

John Spencer Bassett posits that these supposed insurrections may have been fabricated for political reasons by the elites of the state in order to assert a solid pro-slavery stance against abolitionists. And it must be wondered if this was in response to the numerous attempts by Quakers and others to manumit and deport Blacks.[198]

As fears arose from rumors rampant about the state, those who marginally supported the manumission societies withdrew their assent altogether. In a diary entry for October 28, 1831, Quaker Jeremiah Hubbard recalled fears of runaway Blacks hiding in forests after the Nat Turner revolt. It cannot be a coincidence that by 1832, "all the Quaker-supported antislavery societies in the South disappeared," which was also about the same time that the URR began its full service of clandestine escapes.[199]

Thus, it is easy to see how enslavers had their reasons for wanting all Black people removed from the state. Their demand for this policy drove a wedge into the manumission society's ranks. Levi Coffin initially had some reservations about the union. Still, his observations reveal yet another side of Quaker approaches to slavery and attitudes toward slaves.

> *The last convention I attended was held at General Gray's in Randolph County....Quite a number of slaveholders were present who favored gradual manumission and colonization. They argued that if slaves were manumitted, they must be sent to Africa....A motion was made to amend our constitution, so that the name of our organization would be "Manumission and Colonization Society": This produced sharp debate. Many of us were opposed to making colonization a condition of freedom, believing it to be an odious plan of expatriation concocted by slave holders, to open a drain by which they might get rid of free negroes, and thus remain in more secure possession of their slave property. They considered free negroes a dangerous element among slaves. We had no objection to free negroes going to Africa of their own will, but to compel them to go as a condition of freedom was a movement to which we were conscientiously opposed and against which we strongly contended.*

When the vote was taken, a small majority voted for the change. Frustrated that the enslavers and those who supported them had "got the ascendency in our Society," the Quakers pulled out and began meeting at New Garden Meeting instead of Centre and Deep River Meetings, which were in the heart of the enslavers' farms and plantations. Despite the division, in 1817 North Carolina Friends demonstrated their agreement with the Colonization Society by petitioning the North Carolina General Assembly to endorse the plan, and a year later the Friends contributed $1,000 to the Society.[200]

The North Carolina Manumission Society slowly overcame the rift, and by 1827 there were forty societies meeting in the Piedmont area. Northern Quaker Meetings were requested to donate to the cause to supplement the $2,000 that Tarheel Quakers had collected to deport freed Blacks. Northern Quakers rose to the cause and sent $12,000 to the Society. The surge in donations, however, was to end quickly due to another rift, this time within the Quaker fold.[201]

There were continuing fits and starts. The Society, led by Springfield Friends member Nathan Hunt, pursued the "Free Produce" movement. The objective was to set up local stores to sell only products produced by free labor, not slaves. Stores that sold slave-produced goods were to be boycotted. The effort was well-intended, but many came to realize that much of the substitute products were deficient in quality or exorbitantly overpriced. Still, some lived out their convictions in Quaker simplicity. Richard Mendenhall refused to wear clothing that was processed with slave-produced dyes like indigo.[202]

As members of the manumission society like Baptist minister Amos Weaver urged more political action, Quakers, typically averse to political involvement of any kind, questioned this effort. There were growing fissures between those who demanded immediate abolition and those who preferred the measured pace of gradual manumission. In an 1838 letter, Harriet Peck, a teacher at New Garden Boarding School, lamented the overwhelming presence and influence of colonizationists to the minority of abolitionists. The sentiment of William Hockett of Centre Meeting in 1848 revealed two different geographic approaches to enslavement, those highly opposed in Indiana and those who had turned seemingly apathetic in North Carolina. He resigned himself that Friends in North Carolina "seem to adhere in good degree to what I think the best policy, not Clamorous in the Cause but trying to convince the public mind of the inconsistency of slavery with the Christian religion, and when the public mind has been convinced by reason, remonstrance, etc [*sic*] the work of emancipation will be consummated."[203]

Undaunted, individual Quaker members of the North Carolina Manumission Society contributed to the cause. Phineas Albertson of Springfield Friends managed the overseas transport of slaves, and in 1829, he and Nathan Mendenhall escorted Blacks to Norfolk for their eastern journey on the *Nautilus* to freedom.[204]

Still, six hundred of the nine hundred owned by the North Carolina Yearly Meeting trustees awaited liberation. Some were part of lawsuits that involved heirs contending wills. Enslaved relationships were complicated, and while freedom seemed preferable, logical, and practical for whites, it was not the case among bondsmen and bondswomen. Often the spouse of one "freed" Quaker slave was owned by a non-Quaker, thus emigration was refused to remain close to this loved one. Children complicated the matter further. While a parent may wish for a child's freedom, the same parent may decline her freedom to remain near her children or grandchildren. This scenario was not unfamiliar, as noted by Harriet Jacobs in her chilling biography.[205]

To make matters worse, freed family members might agree to emigrate only to refuse at the last minute. Did the frustrated Quakers really understand the complexities of removal that their slaves faced? Frederick Douglass answered no because free people enjoyed mobility and thus held "no extravagant attachment to any particular place." But the enslaved has no say in his/her home. The slave "is pegged to a single spot, and must take root here or nowhere. The idea of removal elsewhere, comes, generally in the shape of a threat, and in punishment of crime. It is, therefore, attended with fear and dread." Closer to home, Moses Grandy, a North Carolina former enslaved who bought his freedom, put it quite succinctly: "As to the settlement of Liberia on the coast of Africa, the free coloured people of America do not willingly go to it. America is their home." Why was America their home? Reverend Thomas Jones, enslaved forty-three years in North Carolina, narrowed it down further. "I can testify, from my own painful experience, to the deep and fond affection which the slave cherishes in his heart for his home and its dear ones." In the eyes of idealistic abolitionist whites, freedom was the most important aspect for the enslaved, but for the enslaved themselves, while all dreamed of it, for many, removal, while well-intended, was simply another form of enslavement to white control.[206]

There were other impediments as well. The Yearly Meeting allotted up to $200 per bondsperson for expenses in traveling, including food, shelter, and clothes, but these funds did not grow on trees. Some enslaved were obstinate and, asserting their newfound freedom, refused to go unless they could choose their new place of residence. Other slaves, aware of bad stories of travels to, and the travails in, Liberia, refused to leave their Quaker home. Conditions in Haiti were no better, leading to tensions between the North Carolina Yearly Meeting and the Haitian government. And some enslaved were just lazy or unprepared for the farming life in Africa or Haiti. The end result was enslaved peoples who refused to leave for freedom or even returned to North Carolina continued to cost Friends. Losing their storied patience, Quakers became more and more frustrated with those who simply refused to go anywhere and thus continued living on the dole of their generous benefactors. To the whites, including some Quakers, they were deemed lazy and dependent.

ONE UNEXPECTED ISSUE AROSE for the North Carolina Yearly Meeting in 1836. Some formerly enslaved who had been taken to New York City, a month later, decided to come back to Pasquotank. Indeed, Quaker David White, who led several groups of freed slaves to Indiana, Pennsylvania and New York, was incensed that these freed people had actually planned this deed before they left North Carolina. Such a scheme meant that they would be exposed to numerous perils and threats, even death, if caught on their journey home. Not to mention it cost money to bring them back. What on earth would make a freed person plan this at all?[207]

Slaves were not as ignorant of racial issues as many, both then and now, might have assumed. It is certainly plausible that they knew very well that New York City, indeed, the North in general, was not as amenable to freed slaves as apparently some Quakers believed. Even in the 1850s, William, uncle to Harriet Jacobs, did not feel safe enough in New York to settle down. He looked farther northward to find full freedom. Indeed, the rising wealth of many New York City citizens depended on the labors of the enslaved. And the city was no stranger to racism and brutal treatment.[208]

Indeed, by the 1820s, Northern states were increasingly becoming hostile to the rising numbers of Blacks crossing their boundaries. Ohio and Indiana were the first to respond to this growing racial crisis. In 1829, Ohio officials decided to enforce an 1809 law that required any Black person in the state to post a $500 bond. Blacks in the state had thirty days to post the bond. Since the North Carolina Yearly Meeting allotted only $200 per slave, this would be an enormous financial burden for them. Blacks who could not post the bond had one alternative: leave the state. But if Northern states were increasingly hostile against all Blacks, where could they go? Since Canada was open to all peoples, that became the new destination for freedom. Within a year, over one thousand Blacks left for the North. Indiana followed suit in 1831, requiring both a $500 bond and proof of freedom.[209]

With Indiana and Ohio now being out of the picture for free Black people from North Carolina, Tarheel Friends looked to Pennsylvania as a destination. In one instance, Jonas Mace, or possibly Benjamin Mace, cared for forty to fifty freed Blacks, all technically held by the Yearly Meeting. The burden was too much to bear, so it was planned to take them to Haiti. They hired the *Julius Pringle*, but the ship wound up taking its ninety-two passengers to Pennsylvania, not Haiti. More confusion followed. Frustratingly, at the same time, Pennsylvania Friends, through a letter from

Edward Bettle, warned against this effort, citing two reasons: first, the influx of Blacks would move Pennsylvania to enact laws similar to those of Indiana and Ohio, and second, it would accelerate rising resentment toward Blacks already in the state. There was a third factor: since the Nat Turner revolt in 1831, former enslaved peoples had fled the South as fears of a massive Black uprising grew among whites. Pennsylvania was the destination for many of these freedom seekers.[210]

When the *Julius Pringle* arrived in Pennsylvania in June 1832, it was met by an angry mob that, ironically, included Quakers, who tried to deny the Black freedom seekers entry. Eventually, they were transferred to another ship and taken to Africa. But with the increasing financial woes of the American Colonization Society and increasing abolitionist attacks against the Society, Africa was no longer a destination of freedom. What would North Carolina Friends do?

In 1834, Jeremiah Hubbard and Phineas Nixon left North Carolina and made personal appeals to the Meetings for Sufferings in the Baltimore, Pennsylvania, New York, and New England Yearly Meetings. The response they received was disheartening: there were rising resentments against Blacks in the North, thus North Carolina should refrain from sending slaves northward. In a conciliatory move, Northern Friends were happy to contribute funds for freedom, but again, where was this freedom to be had if the North was hostile to Blacks? Perhaps they meant freedom in Africa or the West Indies. This put the North Carolina Yearly Meeting in a quandary. Still the owners of "Free Negroes," they needed to quickly find them new homes in "free" states. A letter from Ohio Friend Isaac Parker encouraged them to reconsider taking them west. He noted that the Ohio Meeting for Sufferings could not officially offer safe haven or even encourage the importation of free and fugitive Blacks but that individual Friends might be willing to help small groups. The North Carolina Yearly Meeting now saw an opportunity. No doubt realizing that a significant portion of its members had moved to the Northwest, it decided it would resume sending Blacks there regardless of the legalities. In October 1834, 133 Black people, divided into three groups, were escorted to Ohio and Indiana. In 1835, a second group likewise left for freedom. Individual Friends took them under their care, providing land and apprenticeships for their new neighbors.[211]

The North Carolina Meeting for Sufferings emancipated around 1,100 formerly and currently enslaved over a thirty-year period. As Opper concludes, the Friends wanted to be an example for other North

Carolinian enslavers but they did not—indeed, could not—pursue the overwhelming task of freeing all bondspeople in the Tarheel State. That would be left to others.[212]

John Spencer Bassett sums up the work and frustrations of the North Carolina Quakers at this point: "Whatever the vitality it had left seems to have been thrown into support of the Underground Railroad."[213]

An announcement in the December 23, 1830 *Roanoke Advocate* said it all:

> *People of Color.—The Society of Friends have removed from North Carolina 652 persons of color from under their care, and an unknown number of children, husbands, and wives that were connected with them by consanguinity—In doing this, the Society have expended twelve thousand, seventeen hundred and sixty nine dollars, fifty cents. There are remaining in their care, four hundred and two.*[214]

QUAKERS AND THE MARITIME RAILROAD

My father was an engineer and towed vessels in and out of the Wilmington harbor… Father enjoyed the friendship of two very distinguished Quakers, Mr. Fuller and Mr. Elliott, who owned oyster sloops, and stood at the head of what is known in our country as the underground railroad…Father having a foretaste of liberty to some extent, and growing weary of the life of a slave, with the assistance of his Quaker friends plans were laid for him to purchase his own freedom and go to Canada.

—*William H. Robinson,* From Log Cabin to the Pulpit, or, Fifteen Years in Slavery *(1913), 13*

As the previous chapter points out, the well-intended efforts of conscientious Friends in North Carolina were met with numerous frustrating dead ends. Despite the coordinated efforts of Quakers and others, the North Carolina Manumission Society and the Meeting for Sufferings were not fulfilling their goals. Writing in 1902, North Carolina historian Sallie Stockard, a friend of Addison Coffin, whose family was at the center of the URR in Guilford County, detailed the next step:

> *The Underground Railway, though in reality an outgrowth of the Manumission Society, was not connected with it. This was a secret organization begotten in the ingenious brain of the Coffins, by which slaves were sent to the Northwest.…The first "depot" of this "railroad" was in southwest Guilford County, not many miles from the Randolph*

> *County line. The negro escaped from his master at night, went to one of these "agents," was concealed by day in the hiproof of his house; by night he was sent to the next "agent's" home, and so to free territory. A system of nails driven in trees along the way marked which fork of the road to take.*[215]

Her brief description of the machinations of the URR are quite familiar to most of us and are what we ascribe to Quakers. However, the story of Quakers and the URR in North Carolina is much more complex.

Before there was an *underground* railroad in North Carolina, there was the *maritime* railroad, and it continued right up to the Civil War. As late as 1856, the *Weekly North Carolina Standard* of Raleigh lamented that many "valuable slaves" had escaped from Bertie County, in this instance by the maritime railroad. One modus operandi was that a free man of color on a ship from the North would locate and assist a slave to escape. This particular incident occurred near Plymouth.[216]

In colonial North Carolina, years before the Civil War, runaways initially had only two paths for freedom. First, they could head east to the coast in hopes of catching a ship bound for another world. This is what historian David Cecelski calls the *maritime railroad* (MRR). Later, as North Carolina runaway slave ads indicate, in the Piedmont, they might head east, south, or even north to Virginia, sometimes to live once again with their previous master. Many North Carolina enslaved absconded to Virginia (probably to the ports of Norfolk or Portsmouth) or to the North Carolina coast before about 1820. Important for the next chapter, this year coincides with about the time that North Carolina Quakers began moving northwest to escape Southern enslavement.[217]

Lester Craig Cannon Jr., in a vague note about coastal Carteret County Quakers, recalls that "many Quakers here actually gave assistance to the Underground Railroad." He does not elaborate further, and since many—if not most—Quakers had fled the enslaving culture of coastal North Carolina at the time suggested by Cannon, this recollection could just be a generalized statement frequently found in Friends' reminiscences. Addison Coffin provides more details for us: "In eastern North Carolina where water transportation was used, they had secret channels and byways, marked…by different means known alone by their boatman."[218]

William H. Robinson, a former enslaved person from Wilmington, North Carolina, penned a memoir that included stories about his father, Peter. Peter was enslaved by a shipowner and farmer who enslaved five hundred others. Peter, an engineer and pilot, towed ships entering the port and navigated the treacherous waters of the Cape Fear River. Peter, "by constant contact with white men," made friends with two "distinguished Quakers, Mr. Fuller and Mr. Elliot," whose trade was in oysters. "They stood at the head of what is known in our country as the underground railroad.... Hundreds of men belonging to this organization sacrificed their lives in carrying out this noble purpose." No doubt these Quaker merchants relied on their ties to Northern Quakers to carry out these plans. New Bedford, with a large population of Quakers and freed Blacks, was one of many ports with ties to the South.[219]

The distinction between the underground and maritime railroads is a recent one. Robinson, writing many years after his early days in Wilmington, discusses the methods of the *underground* railroad, not the *maritime* railroad. He recalls that the area was divided into regions with stations or depots every fifteen to twenty miles apart. "One man would haul the slaves at night to the end of his station and get back home before daylight, undetected." Fugitives were carried in wagons that "had a double lining with corn or wheat visible, while the cavity was filled with women and children." Curiously, he does not describe the ways of the watermen.[220]

Peter towed Fuller's and Elliot's sloops day in and day out, and their conversations did not just focus on nautical problems. They also discussed ways to secret runaways to freedom in Canada. The two men also devised a way for Peter to purchase his freedom.

The 1840s were filled with such escapes, and by 1849, Blacks escaped through this MRR every day. Helped by people like Peter who would find co-conspirators in others, including whites, fugitives fled the North Carolina ports in droves. The work was dangerous, and those who were caught faced serious consequences. Fortuitously, years later, William ran into the son of one of the Quakers, Sam Fuller Jr. Fuller related that his father, Sam, was one of the Quakers who worked with Peter. When the plan was discovered by Peter's owner, Peter was captured and sold to slave traders, and then Sam Fuller was confronted at night and told to leave the state. He did so, leaving behind his wife and four children. Sam Fuller was never heard from again, and word was he was hanged.[221]

While 70 percent of freed enslaved narratives mention maritime escapes, stories about maritime fugitives receive little if any attention in classroom discussions and even publications. The MRR existed in the late 1700s, decades before the more organized inland URR. In 1795, Virginia officially recognized "what were shadows of a secret network formed to assist in the absconding of slaves." Before the thirteen proslavery colonies were united into one nation, there were no Northern free colonies to which to flee. Thus, the only way out of enslavement was to head to the coast and hope to catch a ship headed away from North Carolina. Early runaway slave ads are filled with notices that projected fugitives were heading east to a port. For example, the Virginia port of Norfolk was one destination for North Carolina slaves, as was any major port on the North Carolina coast. These included Elizabeth City, Edenton, Bath, Beaufort, New Bern, Washington, and Wilmington.[222]

Maritime North Carolina enslaved enjoyed much more freedom than the enslaved who labored on farms deeper in the state. An enslaved man might pilot a barge from an inland plantation down a waterway to a town port, spend days there while the cargo was unloaded, and then head back home, a journey of possibly several weeks. While farm life was difficult for the enslaved inland, there was more free time for maritime bondsmen and bondswomen to make baskets, grow vegetables for sale locally, fish and sell their catch, or hire themselves out for local work. Those with specific skills would be hired out for the shipbuilding industry. On the wharves and sidewalks, they typically sold their wares to local shoppers to make some extra money. In fact, amazingly, many enslaved sold to inland farmers often returned to their former owners. Numerous North Carolina runaway slave ads warn the fugitive might be on his way back to the coast and his former owner or a wife or family.[223]

The enslaved and freed Blacks formed an informal news network along the rivers, estuaries, and ports. As William Robinson recalled, "To get news from one farm to another one slave would tell the other, and so on, until by this means and that of the underground railroad, it would reach its destination." As ships arrived, crew members would divulge stories and news from far away. Blacks who worked the ports shared these stories among themselves and up the rivers. Enslaved watermen who floated barges and boats up and down the waters brought this news back to the plantations. As inland enslaved people traveled to other plantations for family visits on Sundays, news was shared and spread even farther west. And the enslaved sold to farmers deep in the state would share these stories as well. Thus, a "long, complex web of informants, messengers, go-betweens and other potential collaborators" ran from the coast to farms, sometimes even to the western part of the state. And much of this lore involved the tales of ships taking fugitives north to freedom. Blacks within this system also knew who was sympathetic toward the runaways, both white and Black, enslaved and free. And some of these benevolent souls were Quakers.[224]

The MRR was not restricted to the coast and inland waterways. In 1828, Nathan Mendenhall, who was associated with the Piedmont Deep River and Jamestown Meetings, accompanied free Blacks to Norfolk, where they embarked on the *Nautilus* for Liberia. Interestingly, this story was published in the 1829 *Friend* magazine, so Mendenhall's reputation would have been public knowledge. John Stafford of Cane Creek meeting, along with Levin Wood, cared for ten enslaved whose owner desired to liberate them. In 1826, they were taken to Haiti.[225]

Phineas Nixon Jr., a Quaker who lived in the Caraway community of Randolph County, as power of attorney, accompanied freedmen out of Beaufort in 1826 to Haiti. They embarked on the *Sally Ann* for the month-long voyage. After paying port fees and other expenses, Phineas turned in a bill for $500 for his journey, demonstrating just one of the many costs involved in carrying freed people to a new life. In 1826, George Swain of Deep River Meeting escorted ex-enslaved to Beaufort, via Wayne County, where he picked up more freedmen from local Quakers. When he discovered that the captain and first mate were taking on more cargo, meaning less space for his wards, he questioned the move. Racist language from the captain and his mate ensued. He then went to the owner of the *Sally Ann* and demanded the captain and first mate be removed or else he would cancel the voyage. His demand was met. It is no wonder that the enslaved often sought help and advice from this tenacious and intimidating Quaker.[226]

Some ships and their captains were more involved in this dangerous maritime escape route than others. The schooner *Sally Ann* sailed the waves of the MRR numerous times in its transport of ex-enslaved and runaways. Not all trips were successful, as one sad story reveals. One schooner arrived in Boston in 1854 with fugitives hidden in the hold; they were discovered by local authorities. By law, the hapless captives were to be jailed and then deported to the South.[227]

Quakers in North Carolina played their part in this maritime scheme, but not all of it was clandestine. There was another form of "railroad" in which freed Blacks and even some slaves escaped in plain sight. And it was not just Blacks who wanted to escape the slave South. Quakers were fleeing enslavement, both theirs and of others, as well.

QUAKERS AND THE ABOVEGROUND RAILROAD

Slavery and Quakerism could not prosper together, and many of the Friends from New Garden and other settlements moved to the West.
—Levi Coffin (1880), Reminiscences, *76*

Slaves weren't the only ones seeking freedom from slavery. As noted in previous chapters, Quakers realized that slavery was leading them away from their original beliefs as taught by founder George Fox. In essence, they were enslaved to the lavish and ever-lazier lifestyles that enslavement produced for them. Quakers fleeing their bondage to the enslaving culture in North Carolina often brought fugitives as well as "Free Negroes" with them on what is called today the Aboveground Railroad (ARR).

Roger Kirkman makes a brief note about Westfield Friends Meeting in Surry County: "As one of the main stations on the Underground Railroad, which includes Westfield, Fort Chiswell, Charleston, Point Pleasant, Chilicothe, Xenia, Dayton, Richmond, and Westfield, [it] occupied a unique strategic position in the operations of the Manumission Society." There is no mention of any URR activities in Westfield's histories, so this note seems incorrect. And the names listed here are not other meetings in North Carolina. They are, however, *towns* on a route from Westfield Meeting through Virginia, what is now West Virginia, and Ohio and Indiana.[228]

This is the exact route taken by migrating Quakers who fled the enslaved culture of North Carolina for the new life in the Northwestern Territory of the new nation. Quaker historian Seth Hinshaw states unequivocally that, in North Carolina, "Friends saw the slave society as corrupt and corrupting, and they feared its corrosive influence on their way of life, and especially upon their children." As they rode north and west over old buffalo trails—buffalo used to migrate south to winter and then back north for the summer—they may not have realized what they were headed toward. With hopes of escaping their enslavement to slavery and dreams of yet another new beginning, the peculiar institution would follow them and continue to haunt them and force the "construction" of further tracks and stations into Canada.[229]

"Conductors" in this very open railroad include names of Quakers we have previously met: Asa Folger, Joseph Hunt, David White, John White, Joseph Stafford, John Fellow, Joseph Harris, Robert Peele, Thomas Outland, and Miles White. Others involved in the ARR were Thomas Kennedy, Thadeus White, Phineas Nixon, Jonas Mace, and Isaac White. Sometimes the trip was nearly impromptu. When Nathaniel Newlin's brother Thomas was visiting from Indiana, Nathaniel purchased an enslaved Black man, Jim, from Caleb Guthrie in Alamance County. Jim then accompanied Thomas back to Indiana.[230]

Thus, what we have called the URR was not just clandestine knocks on doors in the night but an open, aboveground movement of freed and even fugitive slaves by Quakers who were migrating out of North Carolina. As North Carolina Friends exited their home state, Blacks, enslaved and free, often accompanied them.

"The first considerable movement of Friends from North Carolina direct to the West…came from the Contentnea Quarter. It was emphatic and sweeping in its character. It was literally a migration," Stephen Weeks concluded over a century ago. Deliberations concerning such an upheaval of coastal North Carolina Quakers began as early as 1799. Frustrated Friends embarked for Ohio by way of Pennsylvania the next year. Whole meetings packed up their belongings, and in a few short years, Friends meetings in "Carteret, Beaufort, Hyde, Craven and Jones counties were depopulated of Quakers and the meetings laid down [closed]."[231]

Core Sound Meeting was the central point for eastern North Carolina Quakers, and migrations also commenced there in 1799. Afterward, there was a slight lull until migrations westward renewed in 1831. As these Quakers exited, some of the meetings were "kept up by old negroes alone." Wagonloads of Friends rolled westward—especially between 1823 and 1832—and many left their "old negroes" behind to fend for themselves.[232]

In the northeastern portion of North Carolina, the Eastern Quarter of Quakers likewise headed for new homes, but many initially settled in Guilford and Randolph Counties among the large Quaker population there from 1800 to 1810. Disappointed that the curse of enslavement had followed them to the Piedmont, the Eastern Quarter Friends aimed their wagons farther west to Ohio and Indiana for a new life.[233]

Overall, many of these statewide migrations involved large numbers of local Quakers, thus depleting and, in some cases, decimating the membership rolls of meetings throughout the Old North State. Indeed, the very existence of the North Carolina Yearly Meeting was threatened as nearly three-fourths of their meetings were laid down. By 1813, enough Friends lived in Ohio to form a meeting, and one resident, in a fit of hyperbole, claimed that Quakers made up half of the population in the West. By 1850, Quaker Addison Coffin believed that one-third of Indiana was composed of North Carolina Quakers. One significant result of this loss was that it left fewer Quakers to challenge the institution of slavery in the Tarheel State.[234]

Interestingly, some Quakers left their local meetings because their own people would not follow the advice of Quaker leaders and manumit their slaves. Such was the case in Goldsboro. Quakers from the Core Sound Meeting settled in Wayne County beginning in 1741. Soon there was a substantial Quaker population, and some of the Quakers, like Richard Cox, owned thousands of acres of land and operated several successful businesses. In 1810, "many Wayne County Quakers immigrated to Ohio and Indiana seeking further peace and freedom of worship. Those who owned slaves were promptly dropped from the membership rolls." This clearly indicates that some Quakers still refused to release their bondsmen and women.[235]

Most Quakers fled northwest. Between 1820 and 1840, four hundred Quaker families left the Perquimans area alone for Indiana. In many instances, these families would have purchased the enslaved, a considerable expense, and then brought them along as they journeyed to Indiana, where they were given their freedom. In 1835, intrepid David White personally delivered twenty-six enslaved to Indiana and signed them over to freedom. Some of the slaves were purchased with funds from the North Carolina Yearly Meeting.[236]

Wagon trains of Quakers typically followed what was called the Kanawha route, and many of them carried some "Free Negroes" given to the North Carolina Yearly Meeting with them to their eventual freedom. The Kanawha Trail ran roughly from the Quaker strongholds of Jamestown, Springfield, and New Garden, all near Greensboro, up to today's Hawk's Nest State Park and Beckley in West Virginia, then along the Kanawha River to Point Pleasant on the Ohio River, ending in Gallipolis and freedom. Levi Coffin describes an alternate route that many preferred called the Kentucky Road: "Kentucky road, crossing the Blue Ridge at Ward's Gap, crossing New River near Wythe Court-House, Virginia, thence by way of Abingdon, crossing Cumberland River near Knoxville, thence over the Cumberland mountains and through Kentucky to Cincinnati, Ohio."[237]

It was expensive to carry enslaved and free Black people on these migrations. The cost for a thirteen-wagon exodus was well over $2,000. In 1825, the North Carolina Yearly Meeting notified all meetings that funds were needed "to assist the people of color, under Friends care, in the migration to free governments." The goal for the Yearly Meeting was $1,000. Southern Quarterly Meeting was asked to raise $125. Marlboro Meeting, a member of the Southern Quarterly Meeting, was asked to raise $88.54 in 1826 for its part. All in all, it cost $1,093.81 to send sixty-three free Blacks north.[238]

The journey was arduous and dangerous. Wagons broke down, rivers were forded, babies were born, axle-high mud sucked in wagon wheels, and debris maimed oxen hooves. Sore feet needed constant attention, not to mention formidable mountains that had to be climbed, where all pushed wagons a foot at the time. Hostile Indians and bounty hunters lurked in the shadows, as did bears and bobcats. Once in Indiana or Ohio, farms for the now ex-enslaved were often established. Sometimes family migrations were split. The family of Thomas Brookshire of New Garden Meeting is an example. His son William left for Alabama, where he set up a plantation with enslaved Blacks. His daughters Jane, Margaret, and Sarah headed northwest, where Jane's family set up a station on the URR.[239]

Quakers in North Carolina with relatives in Ohio and Indiana used their family connections to ferry Blacks north beginning around the 1820s. Hiram Hilty notes that lists were "drawn up giving the ages of the [slave] emigrants, their former owners, manumission papers if they had them, and any other information that might be needed." Members of New Garden Meeting were the leaders of this form of the ARR in the Piedmont. "Free Negroes" were taken by wagon by conductors on the ARR. These conductors included Joseph Hunt, Asa Folger, Joseph Stafford, Joseph Harris, David White, and Robert Peele. The leaders of these caravans often had power of attorney to handle this "property" when necessary. The Blacks were provided new clothes appropriate for the northern climate sewn by Quaker women. Specially built wagons and strong horses were acquired for the arduous, six-week, nearly five-hundred-mile journey across the formidable Appalachian Mountains.[240]

Quakers throughout the state corresponded with one another to find who was relocating north. Once a family or group of families was located, permission was requested to transport Black people with them. A group from Eastern Quarter had to raise $2,490 to cover the purchase of twelve horses and thirteen wagons that carried 133 Blacks to freedom.[241]

One trick that Quakers employed was the use of false papers. Enslaved persons and Blacks who had been manumitted had to carry papers with them at all times. Papers for freedmen and women included physical descriptions. Runaway slave ads often mention the illegal use of forged passes by runaways. For the Quakers, once a freedman or woman reached the free states, the papers were brought home and reused by a hope-filled freedom seeker who fit the basic physical description. Passes to be used by runaways could also be forged by sympathetic if unethical Quakers. Either method was dangerous. Runaway Moses Roper, in his retelling of his numerous escapes from enslavement in the 1830s, tells of one Quaker east of Salisbury who awaited hanging for forging passes.[242]

Many URR lessons and presentations mention the use of false-bottomed wagons, and we have seen that William H. Robinson recalls such contrivances. Such wagons were employed on these arduous routes as a safety net. While any enslaved with papers could be taken openly, sometimes dangerous situations called for more safety. Fugitives could be hidden in false-bottom wagons at the last minute should trouble arise. Fortunately, one exists in the Piedmont of North Carolina. This relic was originally housed at the Quaker Murrow family farm near Centre Meeting but is currently stored at the Mendenhall Plantation in Jamestown.[243]

According to local lore, this wagon was constructed by Daniel Jones, a local slave and "buggy builder." But there is also another tradition that wagonmaker Frederic Stafford of Cane Creek Meeting may have built false-bottomed wagons, especially after he moved to Guilford County. Since this was nearer to New Garden Meeting, perhaps there was a growing need for such equipment. Some speculate that he made the one now at the Mendenhall Plantation. Joshua Stanley, a member of the North Carolina Manumission Society and Centre Meeting was the original owner of this buckboard wagon. He and his wife, Abigail, adopted two orphans, Joshua's nephews Andrew and Isaac Stanley, and these two drove the wagon. Since they were teens, it was believed they would attract little if any attention from slave hunters. Isaac and Andrew would take slaves in the wagon along the Kanawha route to Ohio or through Wheeling, West Virginia.[244]

There were plenty of wagons without false bottoms in use as well. Eli Haworth of Springfield Friends was a wagon train master who led several groups to Ohio, Indiana, and Illinois. Some of these trains carried as many as thirty families, and each journey took half a year. It was quite common for Quakers to carry "freed" enslaved north on these trips. David White was active in the Meeting for Sufferings and escorted many freedmen and women to Indiana and Ohio. William Manlove of Deep River Meeting purchased a baby at the request of his enslaved mother. The baby boy was treated as an adopted child and at the proper age became a blacksmith apprentice. He stayed with the Manlove family when they moved to Illinois, most likely to avoid being stolen by slave catchers. Joseph Hunt of Springfield Friends was a member of the North Carolina Yearly Meeting for Sufferings and a "prototype" of conductor before the real URR was in operation. In the 1820s, he took several loads of slaves to Indiana.[245]

Sometimes, however, a lone Quaker would take a fugitive on the long journey northwest. Such is the case with Benjamin Millikan of Springfield Friends Meeting. "Emancipator Ben" was a frequent conductor of the URR. He often guided runaways from Springfield to New Garden Meeting, and at least six times he escorted freedom seekers to free states.[246]

Some freed Blacks and fugitives walked to freedom following wagons. Levi Coffin recalls the procedure used by Quakers. Freed Blacks with their manumission papers were generally safer. On the road to Indiana/Ohio, they normally walked some distance behind the wagon in plain sight. After arriving in the free North, the papers would be sent back to North Carolina in hopes that other enslaved people who matched the description might surreptitiously use them again. In another act of subterfuge, the documents of freed people, however, were often copied and signees' names forged. If a runaway met the description of the freed Black in the documents, then he/she was taken along on the journey. Blacks without papers would follow the wagons at night, arriving at the camp of the party before morning to eat and then hiding in the woods during the day. Signals were employed for changes in the road or trail. For example, if there was a fork in the road, a limb or bush or other sign would be placed at the crossing pointing to the direction to take.[247]

The Northwest, however, was not the panacea Quakers and Blacks hoped for. As anti-enslavement advocates in the South, predominately Quakers, schemed to move slaves to the North, racism reared its ugly head. Northerners sought to prohibit both enslaved and free Blacks from entering their states. Ohio passed a law in 1803 to thwart the flow of Blacks and Mulattoes into the state. A few years later, Illinois passed a law to ensure that it would not become a haven for runaways. One after another of the Northern states passed prohibitions to stem the influx of Blacks, enslaved and free, into their territories. In 1820, Missourians adopted a constitution that prohibited free Blacks and people of mixed heritage from entering and settling in their state. Indeed, the North in varying degrees may have stood against slavery, but racism was no stranger to its citizens. Alexis de Tocqueville and William J. Watkins observed that prejudices against Blacks were more rampant, indeed vicious, in the lands of the abolitionists than those of the South. It was this virulent *Northern* racism that led to a more organized system of the URR, and some North Carolina Quakers, especially Levi Coffin, were the engineers in the Southern portion of the train.[248]

As Northern prejudice closed its doors to freedom for Blacks, the Northern version of the URR arose, installing tracks to Canada for eventual freedom. And for Southern Blacks to find this ultimate freedom, rails had to be laid to the North, both inland and by the sea. A few North Carolina Quakers dared to go against their own Friends and construct an "underground" railroad.

QUAKERS AND THE UNDERGROUND RAILROAD

Slaves will go anywhere for freedom.... If they can meet with a man in a broad-brimmed hat and Quaker coat, they speak to him without fear—relying on him as a friend. At each place the escaped slave inquires for an abolitionist or a Quaker, and these friends of the coloured man help them on their journey northwards, until they are out of the reach of danger.
—*Moses Grandy,* Narrative of the Life of Moses Grandy; Late a Slave in the United States of America *(1843), 182–83*

It is known that the northern abolitionists maintain a regularly-organized association, which by means of secret agents in the slaves states and a species of conveyance between the Ohio river and the northern lakes, known as the 'underground railroad,' is engaged in enticing negroes from their masters and running them into Canada.
—*The* North-Carolinian, *November 26, 1853 (republished from the* Louisville Journal*)*

While Quakers fought against enslavement in the courts, by membership, and with actions through the North Carolina Manumission Society, the "Free Negroes" program, and with the ARR and relocation to Haiti, Liberia, and the Northwest, these were mostly efforts to move *free Blacks* to a land of greater freedom. The lack of total success in fighting enslavement in North Carolina led to two final moves by Tarheel Friends. The first we have covered: Quakers removing to free states. The second was the Underground Railroad. Contrary to popular belief, this effort was totally banned by the Society of Friends in North Carolina, as seen in this Epistle of Advice from 1843:

> *Whereas it is a well-known testimony of the society of friends that they do not allow their members to hold slaves or in any way to interfere with the system of…and it having through report come to the body of society that some one or more of the members thereof have suffered themselves to be so far overcome through sympathy to allow and give shelter improperly to one or more slaves and thus occasioned several of their fellow members to be accused of like improper conduct. We have therefore… to make known our long-established practice and utter disapproval of such interference in any way whatever while at the same time we do not in the least degree relinquish our testimony to the injustice of slavery.*[249]

This epistle reveals one of the rare moments when a hint of the URR is made in official North Carolina Quaker records. An intrepid few Friends now fought not only the horrid abuses of enslavement but also the ineffectiveness and even indifference of their own coreligionists in a last-ditch effort to move fugitives to freedom.

In colonial North Carolina, runaways could head east for the MRR. Many North Carolina slaves ventured to Virginia (probably to the port of Norfolk) or to the North Carolina coast before about 1820. By then they might head to, or remain in, the Piedmont and head east, west, south, or even north to Virginia, often to live once again with their previous master or to be around relatives and family. (In the Southwest, freedom seekers even absconded to Mexico.) Some Blacks in the western part of North Carolina fled west to Tennessee (which, in earlier times, was then still part of North Carolina).[250]

The overwhelming majority of fugitive slaves in the Tarheel State used elaborate, well-informed networks of slaves, freedmen, and, occasionally, a few whites to mitigate their flight to freedom. Moses Grandy, himself a former enslaved from Camden County, North Carolina, relates a version of escape that reveals both the pluck of individual fugitives and the help of Quakers:

> *Numbers of my coloured brethren now escape from slavery* [and] *suffer many privations in their attempts to reach the free states. They hide themselves during the day in woods and swamps; at night they travel, crossing rivers by swimming, or by boats they may chance to meet with, and passing over hills and meadows which they do not know; in these dangerous journeys they are guided by the north-star, for they only know that the land of freedom is in the north. They subsist on such wild fruit as they can gather, and as they are often very long on their way, they reach the free states almost like skeletons....If they meet with a man in a broad-brimmed hat and Quaker coat, they speak to him without fear....At each place the escaped slave inquires for an abolitionist or a Quaker, and these friends of the coloured man help them on their journey northwards, until they are out of the reach of danger.*[251]

Sometimes white and Black colluded. In a letter to the Dixon family of Snow Camp, Susan Hubbard described a situation where her father was falsely accused of harboring a fugitive. It turned out that an anonymous Deep River Quaker was approached by a runaway. This Quaker did not know how to respond within the Quaker beliefs, so he requested help from two other Friends, one being Susan's father. They initially recommended hiding the man, but then Susan's father reneged. The runaway was then sent to the Hubbards' home, where he was turned away. He then went to former enslaved man Richard Ladd, where a false freed paper was secured from one of Ladd's brothers. When the matter reached the courts, Richard Ladd fled to Indiana.[252]

AS NOTED IN THE introduction, the Town of Halifax has searched for URR records and stories from the area. This Roanoke River town is a focal point in NC Historical Sites educational curricula. Many fugitives fled to the Halifax region in their efforts for freedom.[253]

Halifax County had one of the largest free Black populations in the state, and the enslaved population often doubled that of the whites. The free Black population might have been due to the Quakers in the area freeing their enslaved or deeding them over to the North Carolina Yearly Meeting. The oft-cited fact that Rich Square Meeting, which was "large in extent," helped three hundred enslaved people to freedom might explain the high free Black population in the area. The history of Rich Square Meeting's beginning as told by Juliana Peele is enlightening.[254]

Formed by settlers from both southeastern Virginia and northeastern North Carolina, Rich Square Meeting was led by several families, including John Copeland and John Peele. The Peeles owned large tracts of land, and Peele's son John and his descendants, "as well as other Friends, owned a significant number of slaves." Family records revealed Peele's family overall owned 180 enslaved who were deeded over to the North Carolina Yearly Meeting beginning in 1809 or sent to Indiana or even Liberia in 1827. Other members of Rich Square Meeting apparently enslaved similar numbers, for Peele concludes: "Doubtless, similar papers could be found in other Friends' families." In this connection, it may be well to state that the aged and infirm generally remained with their former masters. If we take into account the aged and infirm just connected to the Peele family slaves, the number of 300 people of color mentioned in the Halifax materials is easily reached.[255]

Rich Square Meeting was officially against secretly aiding and abetting runaways, but that did not prevent some members from doing so. The Henry and Dorothy Copeland family were members of Rich Square Meeting on the Northampton side of the river across from Halifax. They helped runaways escape and sequestered them in a secret room and a separate attic, hiding as many as seven fugitives at a time. Quakers Isaac and Jane Parker also participated in this dangerous and illegal pursuit by hiding fugitives in their barn. John and Edna Hare likewise hid freedom seekers. Aside from the URR, since most other Quakers in the region had migrated west, perhaps Rich Square members felt a duty to remain until their freed and "aged and infirm" Blacks under their care could be cared for.[256]

THE ROLE OF TARHEEL Quakers, especially the Coffin family in Guilford County, in this clandestine system of safe houses and conductors is legendary. Addison Coffin recalls what most of us have been taught. Nails hammered into trees for directions, limbs placed in forks in roads to point the way, rocks as indicators beside the road. He goes on to note the use of strings with knots tied into them at various points on the string that were reminders of where to turn. (The Incas used a more complex system of knots and strings known as *quipu/khipu*.) Conductors who patrolled the various routes, keeping them clean of debris and ready for the next runaway, risked their lives to help slaves abscond. Most conductors lasted only ten years or less because of the stress.[257]

An 1890s (?) Portrait of Addison Coffin. Artist unknown. *Public domain, Wikimedia Commons.*

But there is one sobering note that is never shared in URR lessons. Addison Coffin reveals that not all freedom seekers who sought out the Quakers were directed to the URR. The Coffins subjected fugitives to a vigorous interrogation to determine if they could endure the rigors and unexpected perils of the journey. Many fugitives failed to convince the Coffins and were sent back home.[258]

A few members of Cane Creek Monthly Meeting in lower Alamance County took part in the dangerous URR. Finley Coble's "safe house" used to be the two-story log home of William Kirkman. The Kirkmans and other locals (and, depending on the date of this story, possibly members of Freedom's Hill Wesleyan Church, which was a quarter mile south of the Kirkman house) provided clothing, bedding, food, "and other items the slaves might need." During the day, runaways hid in a nearby hollow tree. The fugitives were also taught techniques that would keep bounty hunters at bay. For example, onions or turpentine were rubbed on their feet or shoes to throw off hunting dogs. Runaways should eat from spots across a garden, not a whole row. A heavily picked garden was a sure sign of a hungry person on the run.[259]

One mile south from Cane Creek Meeting and just a few hundred yards below the Kirkman house stood Freedom's Hill Wesleyan Church. Runaways were sequestered underneath the building according to local lore. The church's abolitionist pastor Adam Crooks, whose simple attire and long beard led folks to believe he was Quaker, had ties to the Northern arm of the URR. We can safely assume Freedom's Hill Church was part of the Snow Camp URR.[260]

Centre Friends Meeting, a day's walk west from Cane Creek Meeting, was the locus for the North Carolina Manumission Society, but some members also conducted fugitives on the URR. In the 1800s, active member Seth Beeson Hockett's sisters had already migrated to Indiana. On several of his visits to see them, he carried freedom seekers in a false-bottomed wagon.

Centre member Andrew Caldwell Murrow, orphaned at a young age, was adopted by Joshua Stanley, an important abolitionist at that time. Stanley ran a station of the URR that was at the intersection of what is today US 220 and NC 62. Andrew hid fugitives in a haystack located near the Murrow home. In the barn, what looked like a stack of feed was actually a hidden compartment with feed set around it. Andy was also a conductor on the URR who transported slaves to Newport, Indiana. He would ride the road during the day and sell cornmeal and pottery to locals, giving the impression he was a traveling salesman. The runaway followed behind him at night. He stopped at abolitionist stations that were a day's walking distance apart. "He drove from station to station one day ahead of the fugitives and told the owners of the stations how many runaways to expect the next morning." The freedom seekers were hidden at these locations during the day, and then they walked to the next station at night. The wagon Murrow drove was the false-bottomed wagon owned by Stanley. When dangerous conditions were ahead, the runaways were hidden in the false compartment. The ruse worked. Even U.S. marshals at the Ohio River did not find the slaves.[261]

As we have seen, there is also a house near Centre Meeting on land owned by Ron Osborne, whose lineage can be traced back to the original Quakers in England. The original log house was built in the mid- to late 1700s by Quakers on the Quaker Plan style. There is relevant speculation this structure may have been a safe place for runaways. This is certainly plausible since some Centre Meeting members assisted fugitives and were part of the North Carolina Manumission Society.

Just one day's distance north and west from Centre Meeting sits the Mendenhall Plantation in Jamestown with its famous false-bottom wagon that we know was used on the URR. Richard Mendenhall owned a large plantation, and his house has been associated by many with the URR. But Shawn Rogers, director of the Jamestown Historic Society and the Mendenhall Plantation, offers a sobering pause here. He notes that there is no plausible evidence to suggest that Richard Mendenhall's farm was part of the URR. He does discuss the addition of a porch with a roof that was attached to the second-floor walls. In order to attach this roof, the "dead man's door" (furniture was lifted up to this second-floor door because it could not be carried up narrow, winding staircases) was literally cut in half. The top portion was turned into a window while the bottom half became a Dutch door that allowed access to a small space under the roof where, oddly enough, there is evidence of floorboards that no longer exist. This space sounds much like the cramped closet-like quarters that housed Harriet Jacobs for seven years. It also sounds a lot like the "hip roof" that Sallie Hockett described in southwestern Guilford County in a previous chapter. While there is no proof that this hidden space was used to hide fugitives, Rogers notes that there is evidence that an exact duplicate of this space is found in a house four miles from the Mendenhalls, where the family was known to assist escaped Union soldiers from the prison in Salisbury, local Union sympathizers, Confederate deserters, and Quaker conscientious objectors who refused to join the Confederate army and fled to the free states up north.[262]

Along what has been called the Quaker Road, at Springfield Friends Meeting, is a house owned by the Coffin family. Much like the space under the spiral staircase in Ron Osborne's house, this structure has a hidden space underneath a stairwell. As Joshua Brown, pastor of Springfield Friends Meeting, pointed out, there is no definitive proof that this was a hiding place. Given the house was owned by the Coffins, who were major figures in the North Carolina URR, we can certainly assert that it is plausible nonetheless.

The Allen U. Thomlinson farm also served as a station on the URR. Thomlinson was a leader in Springfield Friends Meeting and, like many Quakers, was a successful businessman who had a tanyard, a shoe shop, a harness shop, and a store.[263]

We should also consider the following notes. A few Quaker Meetings often assisted fugitives absconding from their oppressors. For example, Jamestown Meeting helped relocate runaways; Cane Creek Meeting raised funds for the cause and taught former enslaved people the arts of farming and the trades; Marlboro Meeting collected funds to transport "people of color" to Indiana, Haiti, Liberia, and other places.[264]

These meetings and locations form an east–west line of "stations." This "Quaker Road," as some maps call it, ran from Spring Meeting west to Cane Creek Meeting in Snow Camp, farther west to Centre Friends Meeting, and then took a dip southward to Deep River Meeting, past the Mendenhall Plantation in Jamestown and on to meetings farther west. From Centre Meeting, it headed north to Greensboro and New Garden Meeting. Each of these successive locations was a day's journey or less. And there were enough small plantations with "Free Negroes" along the way who could and did aid and harbor fugitives along this route.

According to Quaker Ron Osborn, there was a Quaker, Needham Perkins, his great-great-great grandfather, who was a conductor on the URR from either Contentnea Quarter or Nahunta Meeting in Wayne County. In Needham's younger years, he taught at the New Garden Boarding School, now known as Guilford College. Students at the school used to take food to runaways hiding in the area. Perkins was captured by two locals near his farm, brutally beaten, and left for dead for his involvement in the URR. Miraculously, he survived.[265]

There is also the mention of Guilford County. What was it about Guilford County that drew freedom seekers like Ephraim to run there for freedom? Certainly, it was the Quaker presence in New Garden Meeting, also home to the North Carolina Yearly Meeting. Ads often mention a contingent of "negroes" headed for Indiana from this location. This was most likely some version of the ARR for "Free Negroes" or fugitives that Quakers conducted. Enslavers were quite aware that this type of operation was available for runaways in Guilford County.

As Hiram Hilty points out, New Garden Meeting in Greensboro "was a gathering point for the expeditions going west" for the trip to Indiana or Ohio, which took as much as six weeks. The Coffin family, who many claim began the URR, resided there, and they had family connections to Indiana. And the Meeting for Sufferings in North Carolina began transporting slaves to Indiana in 1826.[266]

During the Great Depression, former enslaved man John Beckwith related to his interviewer stories about his father, who was enslaved near Goldsboro. He recalled that freedom seekers ran away and eventually found freedom in Ohio. At the risk of speculation, one wonders if they had help from local Quakers. Could it have been from Needham Perkins?[267]

Interestingly, there was also a "rail" from Contentnea Meeting running northeast to Piney Woods Meeting in Perquimans through Rich Square Meeting into Virginia and Isle of Wight leading to Norfolk and, from there, freedom.[268]

Levi Coffin came from a long line of Quakers. His family left Nantucket in 1763 and settled in New Garden when his father was ten years old. His parents owned a farm near New Garden Meeting. His parents moved to Indiana in 1825, and he followed them a year later. Before then, at the age of seven, he encountered the "horror of the cruelties of slavery" when he witnessed a coffle of enslaved men being driven down the Salisbury Road. His father, also named Levi, explained the situation, and from that point forward, the young Levi wore the mantle of abolitionist. Other "such instances of man's inhumanity to man" fueled his fight against injustice for the next fifty years.[269]

Runaways often hid in New Garden. Levi, used to feeding the roving hogs and cattle of his family, knew their hideouts and would often feed the hidden fugitives and listen to their stories. Sometimes they came to his door at night for assistance. Aided by his cousin Vestal (both of whom briefly opened a school for Blacks with the consent of some enslavers like nearby Presbyterian Dr. David Caldwell; other enslavers balked and it was soon closed) and trusted local enslaved man Sol, they specifically looked for freed Blacks who had been kidnapped to be sold off in the Deep South. Levi and Vestal would then interview the captured man and get enough information to eventually retrieve him through *legal* means and bring him back home. Sometimes the brave Levi interceded for a runaway. For example, Ede and her child fled the home of the noted Dr. Caldwell, a respected physician and Presbyterian minister who also founded perhaps the first college in the state. She was afraid he was going to give her to his son, who lived far away. This would separate her from her husband. Ede packed a bag with food, took her baby, and fled, living in the woods for several days until her child took sick. Levi took her in and then went to Caldwell, whom he convinced to keep her.[270]

Coffin relates several harrowing tales of escape, all in the years between 1823 and 1826. Jack was enslaved by a man named Barnes in the eastern part of the state. Nearing death, Barnes bequeathed freedom to Jack, but the family contested the will. Jack, knowing of Quakers in New Garden, fled west to the Piedmont and was taken in by local Quaker families. A question arises here: Why didn't he look to Quakers nearby, such as Rich Square Meeting? An answer might be that he stood a better chance of success by going to New Garden Meeting. Plans were conceived to move Jack to a free state. Levi's uncle Bethuel was moving his family to Indiana and planned to camp along the way, following the Kanawha Road. Somehow avoiding the pursuit of a slave catcher, Bethuel's family and Jack eventually made it.

Not all escapes were as successful. Part of this story included the plight of Sam, who was being hunted by the same slave catcher pursuing Jack. Free papers were obtained from a freedman, copied, and then secreted to the migrating family by a local enslaved Black person, with the instructions only to be used in an emergency. Sam was eventually taken to freedom, following a family who drove along the Kentucky road. Sam hid in the

False-bottomed wagon at the Mendenhall Plantation, Jamestown, North Carolina. Cecil Haworth, former minister at Deep River Friends Meeting, stands by the wagon. *Courtesy of Quaker Archives, Guilford College, Greensboro, North Carolina.*

woods during the day and then followed the family at night, eating with them in the morning. Sadly, Sam became lost and was betrayed by a family that took him in. The slave catcher caught up with him and took Sam south, where he was never heard from again.[271]

Thus the story of Quaker enslavement to enslavement ends. But we come full circle as America in general and Quakers in particular set out to reconstruct their nation. From the very inception of Quakerism by George Fox, the Quakers believed that the enslaved should be given an education.

QUAKERS, FREEDOM, AND EDUCATION

Slavery was a bad thing, and freedom, of the kind we got, with nothing to live on, was bad. Two snakes full of poison... The snake they called slavery lay with its head pointed south, and the snake they called freedom lay with its head pointed north. Both bit the nigger, and they was both bad.
—Former enslaved Patsy Mitchner, of Raleigh, (the Great Depression), in Hermence, My Folks Don't Want Me to Talk About Slavery, *75*

I kin read a little, but I can't write. I went to school after slavery and learned to read. We didn't go to school but three or four week a year, and learned to read.
—Former enslaved Louisa Adams (the Great Depression), in North Carolina Slave Narratives, *4*

On the campus of the Snow Camp Outdoor Theatre sits a lone weathered wooden building. Donated by the Quaker Hinshaw family, members of Cane Creek Meeting, the structure was a "colored" schoolhouse built by their ancestors after the Civil War as part of the Quaker efforts to educate Blacks. The old building is nestled between two Quaker meetinghouses that were also relocated to the campus. The scene is a symbol and testament to the long history of Quaker efforts to minister to and take care of Blacks in North Carolina.

Writing just before 1908, North Carolina Quaker Mary Mendenhall Hobbs recalled the impoverished aftermath of the Civil War in the Piedmont. Houses were destroyed by fire or used for firewood, livestock consumed by Yankees and Rebs alike. Tools—those not stolen—were rusted and broken, barns and fences torn down and burned, what was left on the farm leaked, fell apart, or had to be purchased with Confederate money that was useless. There were no crops, no food, no possessions that might be bartered for victuals and supplies. Stores were nonexistent. Roads, bridges, and railroad tracks as well as telegraph lines had been destroyed. Southern towns and cities were demolished as Northern troops looted, pillaged, and burned their way through the Tarheel State. Quaker historian Hiram Hilty summed up the situation well: "Friends felt so overwhelmed by their own problems, that…there was not much left to help others."[272]

Freed Blacks fared worse. Homeless, destitute, with no land, no food, no tools, and little if any education, many returned to their former homes. Others wandered about, looking for relatives. For most, it was a matter of

"Colored" schoolhouse on the campus of the Snow Camp Outdoor Theatre. *By the author.*

learning to survive. A new form of enslavement lay before them: segregation and sharecropping. Their only hope was the "powerful and universal" dream of an education.[273]

In the middle of and despite all this chaos and devastation, Quakers renewed their penchant for educating their children. With help from the Baltimore Association as well as Northern Quaker yearly meetings, Friends rebuilt themselves with the tools of the classroom. Led by former North Carolina Quaker Allen Jay as well as others, schools for education and agriculture were established and reestablished. The bulk of this movement took place in the Piedmont of North Carolina, specifically Springfield Friends Meeting. One of the leaders from Baltimore, Sarah M. Smiley, set her sights on educating freedmen and women. Soon Sabbath schools, weekly schools, academies, and normal schools were organized and built, books purchased, and teachers located. Deep River, Springfield, and Cane Creek Meetings were initial leaders in the Quaker normal school movement.

By 1867, six schools and twenty-one Sunday Schools had been established. Dr. J.M. Thomlinson of Springfield Meeting was superintendent of the Freedman's Schools, and by 1870, fourteen schools had been established with hopes of achieving that many more in the near future. Sadly, these efforts had diminished by 1872, as the Reconstruction era came to a close in America. Still, some Quakers persevered. John W. Woody, who was a leader in the Slater School, also held normal schools for Black educators in the 1880s.[274]

The Blair family of Springfield Meeting was especially instrumental in the education of freed Blacks. In the antebellum period, Solomon Blair defied the state law prohibiting educating the enslaved. After the war, he built a small schoolhouse in what is today High Point that eventually became "the first high school for African-Americans in North Carolina." Benjamin Blair, with the benevolence of Northern Quakers, led the way in "the education and social and religious betterment of the colored people." Several others in the Blair family were also instrumental in the early days of the Slater School, which later became Winston-Salem State University.[275]

Within this inspired educational movement, New Garden Boarding School in Greensboro received funds for renovations and expansion. The school eventually became Guilford College in 1888, but sadly, it did not admit Black students until 1962.

No longer enslaved to enslavement, some Quakers continued what they began in the late 1600s, the edification of the enslaved. North Carolina

Quakers sought to educate not only their own but others as well. As white and Black went back to school, segregation, another form of enslavement, kept them apart.

Still, both opened their textbooks to new chapters in their lives.

NOTES

Introduction

1. Fisher, "Escape!" See also lesson plans for URR activities "Halifax County, The Roanoke River, and Freedom Seeking," https://k12database.unc.edu.
2. "People of Color," *Roanoke Advocate*, December 23, 1830; Weeks, *Southern Quakers and Slavery*, 227, 242; Outland, Sams, and Littrell, *History of Rich Square Monthly Meeting*. Gwen Gosney-Erickson, archivist at Guilford College Quaker Archives, hails from Rich Square Meeting and verified my conclusions.
3. Weeks, *Southern Quakers and Slavery*, vii, 198; Stallings, "Fragments of Quaker History."
4. Soderlund, *Quakers and Slavery*, 173; Weeks, *Southern Quakers and Slavery*, 74; Newlin, *Friends*, 101.
5. Aptheker, "Quakers and Negro Slavery," 331.
6. Soderlund, *Quakers and Slavery*, conclusion, especially p. 185.
7. French, *Born in Blackness*, 200; Washington, *Up from Slavery*, 16; Northup, *Twelve Years a Slave*, 1; Warren, *New England Bound*, throughout; Foner, *Gateway to Freedom*, 18, 29–30; Brent, *Incidents in the Life*, 182ff.
8. Kidd, *George Whitefield*, 121; "Slavery, the Slave Trade, and Brown University," Brown University, https://slaveryandjusticereport.brown.edu; Benezet, Wallace, and Philmore, *Short Account*, 7, his emphasis; Woolman, *Journal of John Woolman*, 9, 29; Hinshaw, *Carolina Quaker Experience*, 30; Soderlund, *Quakers and Slavery*, throughout.

9. Davis, *Problem of Slavery*, 228, 233; Quakers in the World, "Eliminating Slavery"; *Wilmington (NC) Journal*, October 6, 1854; *North Carolinian* (Fayetteville, NC), January 14, 1860.
10. Soderlund, *Quakers and Slavery*, 54.
11. Harrill, "Slavery"; Hinshaw, *Carolina Quaker Experience*, 128–29.
12. Equiano, *Interesting Life*, 89.
13. Soderlund, *Quakers and Slavery*, 17–19.
14. Hilty, *By Land and By Sea*, 6; Butler, *History of North Carolina*, 14–15; Hobbs, "Complex Networks," 25.
15. Ready, *Tarheel State*, 40; Hinshaw, *Carolina Quaker Experience*, chapter 12.
16. Brent, *Incidents in the Life*, 205.
17. Miller and Allen, *Slave Escapes.*

Quakers and Enslaved in Early Colonial Carolina

18. Kay and Cary, *Slavery in North Carolina*, 52, 58.
19. Kay and Cary, *Slavery in North Carolina*, 52, 54.
20. Brickell, *Natural History*, 9–12.
21. Morris, *Dismal Freedom*, 24; Brickell, *Natural History*, 268–69; Taylor, *American Colonies*, 142–43.
22. Brickell, *Natural History*, 272–74; Kay and Cary, *Slavery in North Carolina*, 54. I have found no indications that Quakers in North Carolina treated their enslaved harshly or cruelly.
23. Crow, Escott, and Wadelington, *History of African Americans*, 3; Bassett, *Slavery in the State*, 8.
24. Brickell, *Natural History*, 276, 285.
25. Crow, Escott, and Wadelington, *History of African Americans*, 15–16. In Virginia, servants were treated as poorly as slaves. To be fair, many poor whites lived in similarly dire conditions as did the very early Quaker settlers in the Piedmont. See Coltrane, *Centre Friends*, 47; Taylor, *American Colonies*, 142; Genovese, *Roll, Jordan, Roll*, 533.
26. Morris, *Dismal Freedom*, 25–31.
27. La Vere, *Tuscarora War*, 11; Ready, *Tarheel State*, 53.
28. Ready, *Tarheel State*, 54–57.
29. Ready, *Tarheel State*, 58–59.
30. Ready, *Tarheel State*, 60.
31. Soderlund, *Quakers and Slavery*, 3–4; Marable, "Death of the Quaker Slave," 17–33.

32. Kay and Cary, *Slavery in North Carolina*, 2–4.
33. Ready, *Tarheel State*, chapters 4–5.
34. Crow, Escott, and Wadelington, *History of African Americans*, 4–5.
35. Crow, Escott, and Wadelington, *History of African Americans*, 6.
36. Ready, *Tarheel State*, 62–64.
37. Kay and Cary, *Slavery in North Carolina*, 98–99, 121.
38. Kay and Cary, *Slavery in North Carolina*, chapter 5.

Quakers in Northeastern North Carolina

39. McMullen and Ernst, *House in the Albemarle*. McCarthy, "Quaker Communities," differs from some accounts.
40. McMullen and Ernst, *House in the Albemarle*, 59–69; Fox, *Journal of George Fox*, 643.
41. Interview with Lynwood C. Winslow III of Newbold-White House, April 16, 2024.
42. Mobley, *Way We Lived*, 32–33; McMullen and Ernst, *House in the Albemarle*, 45ff., 70; Butchko, *On the Shores*, 11; Taylor, *American Colonies*, 138.
43. Mobley, *Way We Lived*, 27.
44. Fox, *Journal of George Fox*, 643; McCarthy, "Quaker Communities."
45. La Vere, *Tuscarora War*, 97.
46. Fox, *Journal of George Fox*, 598–99, 601–5.
47. French, *Born in Blackness*, 293.
48. French, *Born in Blackness*, 185–87, 197, 203, 254; Soderlund, *Quakers and Slavery*, 35.
49. "Quakers in Jamaica and Barbados," Quakers in the World, https://www.quakersintheworld.org; Soderlund, *Quakers and Slavery*, 20.
50. Frost, "George Fox's Ambiguous Anti-slavery Legacy."
51. Hinshaw, *Carolina Quaker Experience*, 2–8; Weeks, *Southern Quakers and Slavery*, 47; McMullen and Ernst, *House in the Albemarle*, 34.
52. Tise and Crow, *New Voyages to Carolina*, 87.
53. Smith and Wilson, *North Carolina Women*, 25; Roundtree, "Old Neck Meeting," 24–25; Roundtree, "Quaker Meeting," 67.
54. Butler, *History of North Carolina*, 143–45, 148; Hinshaw, *Carolina Quaker Experience*, 8–9; Hilty, *By Land and By Sea*, 3; McMullen and Ernst, *House in the Albemarle*, 31.
55. Dungy, "Friend in Deed," 8.
56. Olds, "Quaint Doings"; Hinshaw, "Friends Culture," 43.

57. Woolman uses the term *slaves* throughout his *Journal*, thus showing a clear break from Fox's use of *servants*; South, "Quaker Faith"; Piney Woods Friends Meeting, https://www.pineywoodsfriends.org; the topic of the arson of the meetings arose during my April 17, 2024 presentation on Northeastern North Carolina Quakers and Slavery at the Museum of the Albemarle. Attendants there were mixed on the cause and even the dates; McMullen and Ernst, *House in the Albemarle*, 38; Roundtree, "Old Neck," 26–28; Hinshaw, "Friends Culture," 43, 53.
58. Hinshaw, "Friends Culture," 54–55.
59. Hinshaw, "Friends Culture," 58–59.
60. Hilty, *Toward Freedom for All*, 35.
61. Erickson, "Writings of Rowland Greene," 53.
62. Peele, "Founders of Rich Square," 96; Weeks, *Southern Quakers and Slavery*, 135.
63. Outland, Sams, and Littrell, *History of Rich Square*, 7.
64. Outland, Sams, and Littrell, *History of Rich Square*, 7; Peele, "Founders of Rich Square," 96; Erickson, "'This Threatful Cloud of Iniquity,'" 43, 45.
65. Peele, "Founders of Rich Square," 93–97.
66. Kearns, "Quakers, Slavery"; Hermence, *My Folks*, 41. Please note that I was reluctant to relate this story, as no doubt many in the Peele family today will deny it. As we will see, other Quaker families often had one rogue family member who went against the grain of Quaker conscience.
67. Griffin, "Minutes"; Roundtree, "Quaker Meeting," 32.
68. A. Coffin, "Early Settlement," 3, 46; Grellet, *Memoirs*, 62–63.
69. Grellet, *Memoirs*, 147.
70. Cadbury, "Quaker Bibliographical Notes," 44; Crawford, *Having of Negroes*, 29ff, 73–75, 84–86.
71. Weeks, *Southern Quakers and Slavery*, 142.
72. Winslow, "Winslow, Nathan"; Crawford, *Having of Negroes*, 98–99; Morris, *Dismal Freedom*, 118.

Quakers in Core Sound

73. Weeks, *Southern Quakers and Slavery*, 74.
74. Whitaker, "Newport"; Hinshaw, *Carolina Quaker Experience*, 13.
75. Sandbeck and Warshaw, *Beaufort, North Carolina*, 71.
76. "Williams History," 429, 456 manuscript in the collection of the Carteret County Museum, Moorehead City, North Carolina; Mace,

"Borden Family," 187; Warshaw, "William Bordens"; Core Sound Friends, https://jacealexbaker.wixsite.com/coresoundfriends; Cecelski, "Quaker Map."

77. Specht, "Being a Peaceable Man," 40–42; Soderlund, *Quakers and Slavery*.
78. "Joseph Dew Family"; Specht, "Being a Peaceable Man," 45 and note 15.
79. Garner, "Tuttle's Grove," 93–94; Weeks, *Southern Quakers and Slavery*, 228.
80. Walker, *Sailing to Freedom*, 85.
81. Moore, "Quakers in Wayne County."
82. Thomas, "My Quaker Heritage."

Quakers in Piedmont North Carolina

83. Stockard, *History of Guilford*, 6, 13; Auman, *Civil War*, 6; Stockard, *History of Alamance*, 33.
84. Fisher, *Negro Slave Songs*, 41.
85. Weeks, *Southern Quakers and Slavery*, 96.
86. Weeks, *Southern Quakers and Slavery*, 96; Deep River Friends, https://www.deepriverfriends.com.
87. Teague, *Cane Creek*, 72, citing Woolman's *Journal*, 65.
88. Stewart, *Redemption from Tyranny*, chapter 2.
89. Grellet, *Memoirs*, 64–68, 147.
90. Teague, *Cane Creek*, 72–73.
91. Teague, *Cane Creek*, 72–77; Kirkman, *Break Every Yoke*, 600, 607.
92. Hilty, *By Land and By Sea*, 22, 24; Weeks, *Southern Quakers and Slavery*, 262; Hilty, *New Garden Friends Meeting*, 27.
93. Auman, *Civil War*, 20–23.
94. Hilty, *New Garden Friends Meeting*, 27.
95. Pugh, "Quaker Ceramic Tradition," 4, 9; Coltrane, *Centre Friends*, 43–44, 88, 107–13.
96. Weeks, *Southern Quakers and Slavery*, 104, 264; Briggs, "Quaker Plan Houses," 14.
97. Kirkman, *Break Every Yoke*, 210; Haworth, *Deep River Friends*, 18, 41, 101, 124, 152.
98. Newlin, *Friends*, 18–19, 104–08.
99. Brown, Haworth, and Warren, *Springfield Friends*, 2:3–5, 60.

100. Brown, Haworth, and Warren, *Springfield Friends*, 1:19, 35, 62, 85.
101. Humphries, "Migration of Westfield Quakers," 74–75; Weeks, *Southern Quakers and Slavery*, 109.
102. Robertson, "Friends Near the Frontier," 16, 23, 25, 27.
103. Beaty, *Alamance*, xiii.
104. Stockard, *History of Guilford County*, 66; Newlin, *Friends*, 75.
105. Wood, *Empire of Liberty*, 519–23.
106. Wood, *Empire of Liberty*, 526–40.
107. Kirkman, *Break Every Yoke*, 88; Hinshaw, *Carolina Quaker Experience*, 131.

Quakers Against Quakers

108. Woolman, *Journal*, 2, 51–65, 112.
109. Woolman, *Journal*, 72.
110. Woolman, *Journal*, 72.
111. Fischer, *African Founders*, 109; 120–21.
112. Wood, *Empire of Liberty*, 527–31.
113. Stewart, *Redemption from Tyranny*, 28–35.
114. Woolman, *Journal*, 94.
115. Woolman, *Journal*, 100–103.
116. Woolman, *Journal*, 115–16.
117. Woolman, *Journal*, 117–18.
118. Woolman, *Journal*, 209–11.
119. Hobbs, "Complex Networks," 45, 51–52, 56, 64.
120. Brent, *Incidents in the Life*, 53.
121. Crawford, *Having of Negroes*, 73.
122. Crawford, *Having of Negroes*, 73–75.
123. Crawford, *Having of Negroes*, 73–75, 104.
124. Crawford, *Having of Negroes*, 35.
125. Crawford, *Having of Negroes*, 37, 49.
126. Crawford, *Having of Negroes*, 43.
127. Crawford, *Having of Negroes*, 54, 59; Dungy, "Friend in Deed," 18.
128. Crawford, *Having of Negroes*, 84–86.
129. Crawford, *Having of Negroes*, 86.
130. Dungy, "Friend in Deed," 10.
131. Dungy, "Friend in Deed," 12.
132. Crawford, *Having of Negroes*, chapter 9.
133. Hamm, *Quakers in America*, 37.

134. Hamm, *Quakers in America*, 39–45.
135. Aptheker, "Quakers and Negro Slavery," 357–58.
136. Hinshaw, *Carolina Quaker Experience*, 88–89.
137. Auman, *Civil War*, 13.
138. Whatley, "Last Ride"; Auman, *Civil War*, 138; Black and Drury, *Story of the Wesleyan Church*, 48.
139. Black and Drury, *Story of the Wesleyan Church*, 59; Teague, *Cane Creek*, 75.
140. Hinshaw, *Carolina Quaker Experience*, 136; Hamm, "Evolution," 64; *Greensboro Patriot*, August 2, 1851. https://newspapers.digitalnc.org.
141. Israel, "Free Blacks," 29.

Quakers Versus North Carolina

142. Dungy, "Friend in Deed," 5–6.
143. Dungy, "Friend in Deed," 6–7.
144. Hilty, *By Land and By Sea*, 6.
145. Isenberger, *Native Americans*, 264.
146. Dungy, "Friend in Deed," 16, 18.
147. Dungy, "Friend in Deed," 29.
148. Opper, "North Carolina Quakers," 43.
149. Opper, "North Carolina Quakers," 69.

Quaker Free Negroes

150. *North Carolina Slave Narratives*, 47, 139.
151. Beal, "Underground Railroad," 25; Hickey, "Let Not Thy Left Hand Know," 18ff.
152. Hilty, *By Land and By Sea*, 86–90.
153. *Historical Sketches*, 6; Hilty, *By Land and By Sea*, 5.
154. Sandbeck and Warshaw, *Beaufort, North Carolina*, 72; Erickson, "'This Threatful Cloud of Iniquity,'" 43.
155. Kirkman, *Break Every Yoke*, chapter 2, 31.
156. Opper, "North Carolina Quakers," 40-41.
157. See the Digital Library on American Slavery's *People Not Property* project's Slave Deeds records at the Digital Library of American Slavery, http://dlas.uncg.edu/deeds/; Peele, "Founders of Rich Square," 96–97.

158. See the *People Not Property* project's Slave Deeds records online.
159. See the *People Not Property* project's Slave Deeds records online.
160. Humphries, "Migration of Westfield Quakers," 75.
161. Opper, "North Carolina Quakers," 37–41.
162. Opper, "North Carolina Quakers," 40–41; Newlin, *Friends*, 77.
163. Bassett, *Slavery in the State*, 32–33.
164. Crawford, *Having of Negroes*, 59.
165. Hilty, *Toward Freedom for All*, 40.
166. Aptheker, "Quakers and Negro Slavery," 355–56; Eulis, *History of Snow Camp*, 13; Kirkman, *Break Every Yoke*, 269; Jordan, *Slavery and the Meetinghouse*.
167. Weeks, *Southern Quakers and Slavery*, 214; Kirkman, *Break Every Yoke*, 49.
168. Pugh, "Quaker Ceramic Tradition."
169. Franklin, "Free Negro," 241.
170. Israel, "Free Blacks," 19.
171. Israel, "Free Blacks," 20.
172. Beal, "Underground Railroad," 18; Israel, "Free Blacks," 19–21; A. Coffin, "Early Settlement," 45.
173. Opper, "North Carolina Quakers," 42.
174. Opper, "North Carolina Quakers," 42.
175. Opper, "North Carolina Quakers," 43–44.
176. Hatcher, "North Carolina Quakers," 89-90.
177. Northup, *Twelve Years*, 118–20.
178. Hilty, *By Land and By Sea*, 34–36; Hilty, *Toward Freedom for All*, 49.
179. Cannon, *Heritage of Carteret County*, 92; Hilty, *By Land and By Sea*, 36–40; Hilty, *Toward Freedom for All*, 50; Erickson, "Religion," 20. My thanks to James Shields of the African American Cultural Arts and Historical Center for the information about the Black Masons' fraternity in Norfolk.
180. Kirkman, *Break Every Yoke*, 45-49.
181. Hatcher, "North Carolina Quakers," 93.
182. Tocqueville, *Democracy*, 436–37; McDaniel and Juyle, *Fit for Freedom*, 76–79; Allen, "Racial Thought," 56–57.

Quakers and the Meeting for Sufferings

183. Hinshaw, *Carolina Quaker Experience*, 35, 49–50, 75; Hamm, *Quakers in America*, 185.

184. *Narrative of Some of the Proceedings*, 6–7.
185. Hilty, *By Land and By Sea*, chapters 5–6; *Narrative of Some of the Proceedings*, 23ff.
186. Hilty, *By Land and By Sea*, 46.
187. Hilty, *By Land and By Sea*, 46–50. A slightly different account is in Troxler and Vincent, *Shuttle & Plow*, 231ff.
188. Hilty, *By Land and By Sea*, 51.
189. Hilty, *By Land and By Sea*, 33–34, 40, 45–46.

Quakers and the North Carolina Manumission Society

190. McDaniel and Juyle, *Fit for Freedom*, 53–56.
191. Tocqueville, *Democracy*, 438–40; McDaniel and Juyle, *Fit for Freedom*, 56–57.
192. McDaniel and Juyle, *Fit for Freedom*, 58–59; L. Coffin, *Reminiscences*, 75–76.
193. Weeks, *Southern Quakers and Slavery*, 235–37.
194. Hilty, *Toward Freedom for All*, 41. General information about the North Carolina Manumission Society is taken from Kirkman, *Break Every Yoke*, unless noted otherwise.
195. Smith and Wilson, *North Carolina Women*, 100.
196. Kirkman, *Break Every Yoke*, 52, 389–90.
197. Morris, *Dismal Freedom*, chapter 3.
198. Bassett, *Slavery in the State*, 94–97.
199. Kirkman, *Break Every Yoke*, 440; McDaniel and Julye, *Fit for Freedom*, 86.
200. Levi Coffin in Weeks, *Southern Quakers and Slavery*, 236–38; Whatley, "Last Ride"; Opper, "North Carolina Quakers," 44–45.
201. Kirkman, *Break Every Yoke*, 67, 70.
202. Brown, Haworth, and Warren, *Springfield Friends*, 1:19.
203. Browning, "Harriet Peck," 17; Kirkman, *Break Every Yoke*, 123, 142.
204. Kirkman, *Break Every Yoke*, 164, 266.
205. *Narrative of Some of the Proceedings*, 35ff.; Brent, *Incidents in the Life*, 24–25.
206. Delbanco, *War Before the War*, 113; Andrews, *North Carolina Slave Narratives*, 113, 182, 211.
207. Opper, "North Carolina Quakers," 54–56.
208. Wells, *Kidnapping Club*, throughout; Brent, *Incidents in the Life*, 24.
209. Opper, "North Carolina Quakers," 54–56.
210. Hilty, *By Land and By Sea*, 58–59.

211. Opper, "North Carolina Quakers," 58.
212. Opper, "North Carolina Quakers," 58.
213. Bassett, *Slavery in the State*, 70.
214. *Roanoke Republican*, December 23, 1830, https://newspapers.digitalnc.org.

Quakers and the Maritime Railroad

215. Stockard, *History of Guilford*, 48–49.
216. *Weekly North Carolina Standard*, April 2, 1856.
217. Cecelski, *Waterman's Song*, chapter 5; Israel, "Free Blacks," 10–11.
218. Cannon, *Heritage of Carteret*, 92; A. Coffin, "Early Settlement," 3, 44.
219. Robinson, *From Log Cabin*, 11–12; Cecelski, *Waterman's Song*, 121–22, 130; Walker, *Sailing to Freedom*, 25.
220. Robinson, *From Log Cabin*, 13.
221. Robinson, *From Log Cabin*, 11–15; Cecelski, *Waterman's Song*, 121; Cecelski, *Fire of Freedom*, 17, notes that Fuller was hanged.
222. Walker, *Sailing to Freedom*, 1, 22, 85.
223. Cecelski, *Waterman's Song*, throughout.
224. Robinson, *From Log Cabin*, 17; Cecelski, *Waterman's Song*, 136.
225. Kirkman, *Break Every Yoke*, 164, 514, 601.
226. Kirkman, *Break Every Yoke*, 549, 634.
227. Walker, *Sailing to Freedom*, 73; Quigly, "Safe Harbor."

Quakers and the Aboveground Railroad

228. Kirkman, *Break Every Yoke*, 257.
229. Stockard, *History of Guilford*, 49; Hinshaw, *Carolina Quaker Experience*, 139. Gwen Gosney-Erickson, archivist at Hege Library at Guilford College, explained this to me. She noted that these same places are mentioned by Addison and Levi Coffin in their reminiscences on the URR.
230. Hilty, *Toward Freedom for All*, 77–79.
231. Weeks, *Southern Quakers and Slavery*, 256–59.
232. Weeks, *Southern Quakers and Slavery*, 260.
233. Weeks, *Southern Quakers and Slavery*, 260.
234. Hinshaw, *Carolina Quaker Experience*, 14–15.
235. Tieman, "Quakers Influential in Wayne Development," Smith Harper, https://smithharper.org.

236. "Quakers Influential in Wayne Development," Smith Harper, https://smithharper.org.
237. Hilty, *By Land and By Sea*, 70, 88–89; L. Coffin, *Reminiscences*, 60.
238. *Historical Sketches*, 4–6, 43.
239. Kirkman, *Break Every Yoke*, 97, 100, 302.
240. Hilty, *New Garden Friends Meeting*, 33.
241. Hilty, *By Land and By Sea*, chapter 10.
242. Andrews, *North Carolina Slave Narratives*, 53.
243. Hilty, *Toward Freedom for All*, 94.
244. Kirkman, *Break Every Yoke*, 126, 600, 607.
245. Kirkman, *Break Every Yoke*, 403, 445, 499, 658.
246. Kirkman, *Break Every Yoke*, 523.
247. L. Coffin, *Reminiscences*, 60.
248. Delbanco, *War Before the War*, 129.

Quakers and the Underground Railroad

249. Hilty, *Toward Freedom for All*, 90.
250. Cecelski, *Waterman's Song*, chapter 5; Israel, "Free Blacks," 10–11; Baumgartner, *South to Freedom*.
251. Andrews, *North Carolina Slave Narratives*, 182.
252. Israel, "Free Blacks," 22–23.
253. Martin, "River to Freedom"; "Halifax County, The Roanoke River, and Freedom Seeking," North Carolina Department of Natural and Cultural Resources, https://k12database.unc.edu.
254. Weeks, *Southern Quakers and Slavery*, 88.
255. Peele, "Founders of Rich Square Meeting," 96–97.
256. Weeks, *Southern Quakers and Slavery*, 242; Erickson, "Religion," 21.
257. A. Coffin, "Early Settlement," 3, 44; Hamm, "Addison Coffin." Note that Quaker historian Thomas Hamm has raised questions about the veracity or accuracy of Addison Coffin's recollections.
258. A. Coffin, "Early Settlement," 3, 45.
259. Teague, *Cane Creek*, 74.
260. Crooks, *Life*, 17, notes that he had connections to the URR in Ohio.
261. Coltrane, *Centre Friends*, 111–13.
262. Rogers, "Mendenhall Plantation."
263. "The Freedom Stone," Springfield Friends Meeting, https://springfieldfriends.org; Jay, *Autobiography*, 151.

264. Kirkman, *Break Every Yoke*, 202, 222, 230, 257. Note that I can find no confirmation that Westfield Friends Meeting had any associations with the URR. See the letter by Bertie Dix.
265. Leah, "Secrets."
266. Hilty, *By Land and By Sea*, 68–69.
267. *North Carolina Slave Narratives*, 94.
268. Information from Barbara Gosney as related by the staff at Newbold-White House, April 16, 2024.
269. L. Coffin, *Reminiscences*, 12, 14.
270. L. Coffin, *Reminiscences*, 20–28, 69–71.
271. L. Coffin, *Reminiscences*, 32–64.

Quakers, Freedom, and Education

272. Hilty, *By Land and By Sea*, 94, 106; Hobbs in Jay, *Autobiography*, 128.
273. Crow, Escott, and Wadelington, *History of African Americans*, chapter 5, 81.
274. Hilty, *By Land and By Sea*, 99; Hinshaw, *Carolina Quakers*, 171–72.
275. Brown, Haworth, and Warren, *Springfield Friends* 1:86, 115–16; Hilty, *By Land and By Sea*, 104.

BIBLIOGRAPHY

Digital Sources

Digital Library on American Slavery. "North Carolina Runaway Slave Notices, 1750–1865." https://dlas.uncg.edu/notices/.

———. "People Not Property Slave Deeds." https://dlas.uncg.edu/deeds/.

Publications and Interviews

Albemarle County, North Carolina. "In Ancient Albemarle." https://www.ncgenweb.us.

Allen, J. Timothy. *North Carolina Quakers: Spring Friends Meeting*. Arcadia Publishing, 2011.

Allen, Jeffrey Brooke. "The Racial Thought of White North Carolina Opponents of Slavery, 1789–1876." *The North Carolina Historical Review* 59, no. 1 (1982): 49–66.

Anderson, Jean B., Elizabeth A. Fenn, and Peter H. Wood, et al. "Virginians in the Albemarle: North Carolina before 1770." NCpedia, https://ncpedia.org.

Andrews, William L., ed. *North Carolina Slave Narratives: The Lives of Moses Roper, Lundsford Lane, Moses Grandy, & Thomas H. Jones*. University of North Carolina Press, 2003.

Aptheker, Herbert. "The Quakers and Negro Slavery." *The Journal of Negro History* 25, no. 3 (1940): 331–62.

Auman, William T. *Civil War in the North Carolina Quaker Belt: The Confederate Campaign Against Peace Agitators, Deserters, and Draft Dodgers*. McFarland, 2014.

Bassett, John Spencer. *Slavery in the State of North Carolina*. Johns Hopkins Press, 1899.

Baumgartner, Alice L. *South to Freedom: Runaway Slaves to Mexico and the Road to the Civil War.* Basic Books, 2020.

Beal, Gertrude. "The Underground Railroad in Guilford County." *The Southern Friend* (Spring 1980),

Beaty, Bess. *Alamance: The Holt Family and Industrialization in a North Carolina County, 1837–1900*. Louisiana State University Press, 1999.

Benezet, Anthony, George Wallace, and J. Philmore. *A Short Account of That Part of Africa, Inhabited by the Negroes*. Philadelphia, no publisher or printer, 1762.

Black, Robert, and Keith Drury. *The Story of the Wesleyan Church*. Wesleyan Publishing House, 2012.

Blight, David W. "The Slave Narratives: A Genre and a Source." The Gilder Lehrman Institute of American History, http://ap.gilderlehrman.org.

Brent, Linda. *Incidents in the Life of a Slave Girl*. Edited by L. Maria Child. Introduction and notes by Walter Teller. Harvest Book, 1973.

Brickell, John. *The Natural History of North Carolina*. Johnson Publishing, 1968.

Briggs, Benjamin. "Quaker Plan Houses of Deep River Quarterly Meeting, Guilford County, North Carolina." *The Southern Friend* (Spring–Autumn 1999).

Brown, Joshua, Brenda Haworth, and Dan Warren, eds. *Springfield Friends: 250 Years*. Vol. 1, *The People of Springfield*. Springfield Memorial Association, 2021.

———. *Springfield Friends 250 Years*. Vol. 2, *The History of Springfield*. Springfield Memorial Association, 2021.

Browning, Mary A., ed. "Harriet Peck at New Garden Boarding School, and Her North Carolina Letters, 1837–1839." *The Southern Friend* 26 (2004): 3–55.

Butchko, Thomas R. *On the Shores of the Pasquotank: The Architectural Heritage of Elizabeth City and Pasquotank County*. Museum of the Albemarle, 1989.

Butler, Lindley S. *A History of North Carolina in the Proprietary Era, 1629–1729*. University of North Carolina Press, 2021.

Cadbury, Henry J. "Quaker Bibliographical Notes: II. Antislavery Writings." *Bulletin of Friends Historical Association* 26, no. 1 (1937): 39–53.

Cannon, Lester Craig, Jr. *The Heritage of Carteret County, North Carolina.* Edited by Pat Dula Davis. Hunter Publishing, 1982–84.

Cecelski, David S. *The Fire of Freedom: Abraham Galloway & the Slaves' Civil War.* University of Norh Carolina Press, 2012.

———. "The Quaker Map: From Harlowe to Mill Creek." https://davidcecelski.com.

———. *The Waterman's Song: Slavery and Freedom in Maritime North Carolina.* University of North Carolina Press, 2001.

Clinton, Catherine. *Harriet Tubman, The Road to Freedom.* Back Bay Books, 2004.

Coffin, Addison. "Early Settlement of Friends in North Carolina Traditions and Reminiscences." *The Southern Friend* (Spring 1984).

Coffin, Levi. *Reminiscences of Levi Coffin, the Reputed President of the Underground Railroad; Being a Brief History of the Labors of a Lifetime in Behalf of the Slave, with the Stories of Numerous Fugitives, Who Gained Their Freedom Through His Instrumentality, and Many Other Incidents.* 2nd ed. Robert Clark & Co, 1880. https://docsouth.unc.edu/nc/coffin/coffin.html.

Coltrane, Kay Davis. *Centre Friends: The Legacy of the Meeting on the Hill.* Centre Friends Meeting 2008.

Crawford, Michael J. *The Having of Negroes Is Become a Burden: The Quaker Struggle to Free Slaves in Revolutionary North Carolina.* University Press of Florida, 2010.

Crooks, E.W. *The Life of Rev. A. Crooks, A.M.* Wesleyan Methodist Publishing House, 1875. https://archive.org.

Crow, Jeffrey J., Paul D. Escott, and Flora J. Hatley Wadelington. *A History of African Americans in North Carolina*, 2nd rev. ed. Office of Archives and History, North Carolina Department of Cultural Resources, 2011.

Davis, David Brion. *The Problem of Slavery in the Age of Revolution, 1770–1823.* Oxford University Press, 1999.

Delbanco, Andrew. *The War Before the War: Fugitive Slaves and the Struggle for America's Soul from the Revolution to the Civil War.* Penguin, 2018.

De Tocqueville, Alexis. *Democracy in America.* Bantam Classic, 2004.

Dix, Bertie (Carrol). "A Compilation of Westfield Origins." http://www.surrydigitalheritage.org.

Dodge, David. "The Cave-Dwellers of the Confederacy." *The Atlantic*, 1891. https://www.theatlantic.com.

Douglas, Frederick. *Selected Works.* Fall River Press, 2021.

Dungy, Katherine. "A Friend in Deed: Quakers and Manumission in Perquimans County, NC, 1775–1800." *The Southern Friend* (Spring 2002).

Edmundson, William. *A Journal of the Life, Travels, Sufferings and Labor of Love in the Work of the Ministry, of That Worthy Elder and Faithful Servant of Jesus Christ, William Edmundson, Who Departed This Life in the Thirty First of Sixth Month, 1712*. 2nd ed. Mary Hind, 1774.

Equiano, Olaudah. *The Interesting Life of Olaudah Equiano, or, Gustavus Vass, the African*. Leeds: Craddock and Joy, 1814. In *The Classic Slave Narratives*, edited by Henry Louis Gates. New York: Mentor, 1987.

Erickson, Gwendolyn Gosney. "Religion, Region, and Community Among Women of North Carolina's Eastern Quarter, 1812–1854." *The Southern Friend* (1996).

———. "'This Threatful Cloud of Iniquity': Rich Square Friends and the Challenge of Slavery in 1832." *The Southern Friend* (Spring 2002).

———. "Writings of Rowland Greene During 1832 Visit to Rich Square." *The Southern Friend* (Spring 2002).

Eulis, Juanita Owens. *History of Snow Camp, North Carolina*. Snow Camp Historical Drama, 1971.

Fischer, David Hackett. *African Founders: How Enslaved People Expanded American Ideals*. Simon & Schuster, 2022.

Fisher, Bernard. "Escape!" Historical Marker Database. https://www.hmdb.org.

Fisher, Miles Mark. *Negro Slave Songs in the United States*. Citadel Press, 1990.

Foner, Eric. *Gateway to Freedom: The Hidden History of the Underground Railroad*. W.W. Norton, 2015.

Fox, George, Rev. *The Journal of George Fox*. Edited by John Nickalls. Religious Society of Friends, 1997.

Franklin, John Hope. "The Free Negro in the Economic Life of Antebellum North Carolina: Part I." *The North Carolina Historical Review* 19, no. 3 (1942): 239–59.

French, Howard. *Born in Blackness: Africa, Africans, and the Making of the Modern World, 1471 to the Second World War*. Liveright Publishing, 2021.

Frost, J. William. "George Fox's Ambiguous Anti-slavery Legacy." *Quakers and Slavery*. https://web.tricolib.brynmawr.edu.

Garner, Helen Russell. "Tuttle's Grove United Methodist Church and the Quakers." In *The Heritage of Carteret County, North Carolina*, edited by Pat Dula Davis and Kathleen Hill Hamilton. Carteret Historical Research Association, 1982.

Gates, Henry Louis, Jr., ed. *The Classic Slave Narratives*. Mentor, 1987.

Genovese, Eugene D. *Roll, Jordan, Roll: The World the Slaves Made*. Vintage Books, 1976.

Grellet, Stephen. *Memoirs of the Life and Gospel Labors of Stephen Grellet*. Vol 1. Edited by Benjamin Seebohm. A.W. Bennett, 1860. http://dqc.esr.earlham.edu.

Griffin, Hazel. "Minutes from Jack Swamp Meeting House." *North Carolina Folklore* 11 no. 1 (July 1963) https://digital.ncdcr.gov.

Hamm, Thomas D. "Addison Coffin: Quaker Visionary." *The Southern Friend* (Spring 1996).

———. "Evolution of an Abolitionist: Daniel Worth and the Friends of North Carolina." *The Southern Friend* (Autumn 1980).

———. *The Quakers in America*. Columbia University Press, 2003.

Harrill, J. Albert. "Slavery." *New Interpreter's Dictionary of the Bible*. Abingdon Press, 2009.

Hatcher, Susan Tucker. "North Carolina Quakers: Bona Fide Abolitionists." *The Southern Friend* (Autumn 1979).

Haworth, Cecil E. *Deep River Friends: A Valiant People*. Rev. and updated ed. Deep River Friends Meeting; North Carolina Friends Historical Society; North Carolina Yearly Meeting of Friends, 2009.

Hermence, Belinda, ed. *My Folks Don't Want Me to Talk About Slavery*. John F. Blair, 1984, 1988.

Hickey, Damon D. "'Let Not Thy Left Hand Know': The Unification of George C. Mendenhall." *The Southern Friend* (Spring 1981).

Hilty, Hiram H. *By Land and By Sea: Quakers Confront Slavery and Its Aftermath in North Carolina*. North Carolina Yearly Meeting of Friends, 1993.

———. *New Garden Friends Meeting: The Christian People Called Quakers*. Rev. ed. New Garden Friends Meeting, 2001.

———. *Toward Freedom for All: North Caroliina Quakers and Slavery*. Friends United Press, 1984.

Hinshaw, Seth B. *The Carolina Quaker Experience*. North Carolina Yearly Meeting of Friends, 1984.

———. "Friends Culture in Colonial North Carolina, 1672–1789." *The Southern Friend* (Spring–Autumn 2000).

Historical Sketches of Southern Quarterly Meeting of Friends and Its Constituent Monthly Meetings. North Carolina Yearly Meeting, 1943.

Hobbs, Matthew Wallace. "Complex Networks in Colonial Northeastern North Carolina." Master's thesis, University of Delaware, 1999.

Humphries, Ashley Ellen. "The Migration of Westfield Quakers from Surry County, North Carolina, 1786–1828." Master's thesis, Appalachian State University, 2013.

Isenberger, Daniel L. *Native Americans in Early North Carolina: A Documentary History*. Office of Archives and History, North Carolina Department of Cultural Resources, 2013.

Israel, Adrienne M. "Free Blacks, Quakers, and the Underground Railroad in Piedmont North Carolina." *The North Carolina Historical Review* 95, no. 1 (2018): 1–28.

Jay, Allen. *Autobiography of Allen Jay, (1831–1910)*, edited by Joshua Brown. Friends Historical Press, 2010.

Jordan, Ryan P. *Slavery and the Meetinghouse: The Quakers and the Abolitionist Dilemma, 1820–1865*. Indiana University Press, 2007.

"Joseph Dew Family." Manuscript in The History Museum of Carteret County. Morehead City, North Carolina.

Kay, Marvin L. Michael, and Lorin Lee Cary. *Slavery in North Carolina, 1748–1775*. University of North Carolina Press, 1995.

Kearns, Andre. "The Quakers, Slavery and My Family." *Medium*. https://andrekearns.medium.com.

Kidd, Thomas S. *George Whitefield: America's Spiritual Founding Father*. Yale University Press, 2014.

Kirkman, Roger N. *Break Every Yoke: The North Carolina Manumission Society, 1816–1834*. Telikon Inc., 2016.

La Vere, David. *The Tuscarora War: Indians, Settlers, and the Fight for the Carolina Colonies*. University of North Carolina Press, 2013.

Leah, Heather. "Secret Passageways and Freedom Roads: Remnants of the Underground Railroad in NC." WRAL News, July 26, 2020. https://www.wral.com.

———. "Secrets of Rural North Carolina." WRAL News, February 26, 2023. https://www.wral.com.

Mace, Francis Borden. "The Borden Family." In *Heritage of Carteret County*, vol. 1. Carteret County Historical Society, 1982.

Marable, Manning. "Death of the Quaker Slave Trade." *Quaker History* 63, no. 1 (1974): 17–33.

Martin, Lance. "River to Freedom: Roanoke and Freed Slaves." News From Roanoke Rapids, Weldon and Halifax County, August 14, 2010. https://rrspin.com.

McCarthy, Ann L. "Quaker Communities in Albemarle." Perquimans County, NCGenWeb. https://ncgenweb.us.

McCullough, David. *The Pioneers: The Heroic Story of the Settlers Who Brought the American Ideal West*. Simon & Schuster, 2019.

McDaniel, Donna, and Vanessa Julye. *Fit for Freedom, Not for Friendship: Quakers, African Americans, and the Myth of Racial Justice*. Quaker Press of Friends General Conference, 2009.

McMullen, Phillip S., Jr., and H. John Ernst III, eds. *A House in the Albemarle: English Settlers, Quakers, and the 1730 Newbold-White House*. Pamlico & Albemarle Publishing, 2020.

Miller, Steve M., and J. Timothy Allen. *Slave Escapes and the Underground Railroad in North Carolina*. The History Press, 2016.

Mobley, Joe A. *The Way We Lived in North Carolina*. University of North Carolina Press, 2003.

Moore, Claude. "Quakers in Wayne County." USGenWeb Archives. http://files.usgwarchives.net.

Morris, J. Brent. *Dismal Freedom: A History of the Maroons of the Great Dismal Swamp*. University of North Carolina Press, 2022.

Museum of the Albemarle. "Northeastern North Carolina's Underground Railroad." YouTube, 2019. https://youtu.be.

A Narrative of Some of the Proceedings of North Carolina Yearly Meeting on the Subject of Slavery Within its Limits. Published by Order of the Meeting on Sufferings of North Carolina Yearly Meeting. Swaim and Sherwood, 1848.

Newlin, Algie I. *Friends "at the Spring": A History of Spring Monthly Meeting*. Up. ed. North Carolina Yearly Meeting of Friends, 2016.

North Carolina Slave Narratives from the Federal Writer's Project, 1936–1938. Applewood Books, n.d.

Northup, Solomon. *Twelve Years a Slave*. Barnes & Noble, 2007.

Olds, Fred A. "Quaint Doings of Early Quakers." *Sunny South*, November 2, 1902; https://www.ncgenweb.us.

Opper, Peter Kent. "North Carolina Quakers: Reluctant Slaveholders." *North Carolina Historical Review* 52, no. 1 (1975): 37–58.

Outland, Mary E., Janie O. Sams, and Mary P. Littrell. *A History of Rich Square Monthly Meeting of Friends, 1760–1960*. Woodland, NC, 1960.

Peele, Juliana. "The Founders of Rich Square Meeting." East Carolina University Digital Collections. https://digital.lib.ecu.edu.

Pugh, Hal E. "Quaker Ceramic Tradition in the North Carolina Piedmont: Documentation and Preliminary Survey of the Dennis Family Pottery." *The Southern Friend* (Autumn 1988).

Pugh, Hal E., and Eleanor Minnock-Pugh. "The Quaker Ceramic Tradition in Piedmont North Carolina." Chipstone. https://chipstone.org.

Quakers in the World. "Eliminating Slavery Amongst Quakers." https://www.quakersintheworld.org.
———. "Quakers in Jamaica and Barbados." https://www.quakersintheworld.org.
Quigly, Shawn. "Safe Harbor: The Maritime Underground Railroad in Boston." National Park Service. https://www.nps.gov.
Raboteau, Albert J. *Slave Religion: The "Invisible Institution" in the Antebellum South*. Oxford University Press, 2004.
Ready, Milton. *The Tarheel State: A New History of North Carolina*. University of South Carolina Press, 2020.
Robertson, John Kent. "Friends Near the Frontier: An Account of the Development of the Hunting Creek Friends Meeting, 1794–1828." *The Southern Friend* (Fall 2001).
Robinson, William H. *From Log Cabin to the Pulpit, or, Fifteen Years in Slavery*. 3rd ed. James H. Tift, Publisher, 1913.
Rogers, Shawn M. "Was Mendenhall Plantation an Underground Railroad Station?" YouTube. https://www.youtube.com.
Roundtree, Carlton White. "Old Neck Meeting." *The Southern Friend* (Spring 1997).
———. "Quaker Meeting Near the Narrows of Pasquotank." *The Southern Friend* (Spring–Autumn 1994).
Sandbeck, Peter B., and Mary Warshaw. *Beaufort, North Carolina: African-American History and Architecture*. Eastern Offset Publishing Company, 2021.
Smith, Margeret Supplee, and Emily Herring Wilson. *North Carolina Women Making History*. University of North Carolina Press, 1999.
Soderlund, Jean. *Quakers and Slavery: A Divided Spirit*. Princeton University Press, 1985.
South, Paul. "Quaker Faith: An N.C. Cornerstone." *Virginian Pilot*, November 27, 1997. https://scholar.lib.vt.edu.
Specht, Neva Jean. "'Being a Peaceable Man, I Have Suffered Much Persecution': The American Revolution and Its Effects on Quaker Religious Identity." *Quaker History* 99, no. 2 (2010): 37–48.
Stallings, Olive Rogerson. "Fragments of Quaker History." In *Pasquotank Historical Society Yearbook*, edited by John Elliot Wood. 1958. https://ncgenweb.us.
Stewart, Bruce E. *Redemption from Tyranny: Herman Husband's American Revolution*. University of Virginia Press, 2020.
Stockard, S.W. *The History of Alamance*. Capital Printing, 1900.
Stockard, Sallie W. *The History of Guilford County, North Carolina*. Guilford County Genealogical Society, 1983.

Taylor, Alan. *American Colonies: The Settling of North America*. Penguin Books, 2001.
Teague, Bobbie. *Cane Creek: Mother of Meetings*. North Carolina Yearly Meeting of Friends, 1995.
Thomas, Benjamin. "My Quaker Heritage." *They Lived Along a Rocky River*, https://rockyrivernc.com.
Tieman, Debbie. Wayne County Indiana Government. https://www.co.wayne.in.us.
Tise, Larry E., and Jeffrey J. Crow. *New Voyages to Carolina: Reinterpreting North Carolina History*. University of North Carolina Press, 2017.
Troxler, Carole Watterson, and William Murray Vincent. *Shuttle & Plow: A History of Alamance County, North Carolina*. Alamance County Historical Association, 1999.
Walker, Timothy D., ed. *Sailing to Freedom: Maritime Dimensions of the Underground Railroad*. University of Massachusetts Press, 2021.
Warren, Wendy. *New England Bound: Slavery and Colonization in Early America*. Liveright Publishing, 2016.
Warshaw, Mary. *Beaufort, North Carolina: A Treasury of Significant Town History*. Eastern Offset Publishing, 2019.
———. "William Bordens—Shipbuilders and Colonial Leaders." *More Beaufort, North Carolina History*. http://morebeauforthistory.blogspot.com.
Washington, Booker T. *Up from Slavery: An Autobiography*. Pelican Publishing, 2010.
Weeks, Stephen Beauregard. *Southern Quakers and Slavery: A Study in Institutional History*. Johns Hopkins, 1896.
Wells, Jonathan Daniel. *The Kidnapping Club: Wall Street, Slavery, and Resistance on the Eve of the Civil War.* Bold Type Books, 2020.
Whatley, L. McKay. "The Last Ride on the Underground Railroad." *Notes on the History of Randolph County*. https://randolphhistory.wordpress.com.
Whitaker, Garland R. "Newport—A Home in the Hinterland." In *The Heritage of Carteret County, North Carolina*, edited by Pat Dula Davis and Kathleen Hill Hamilton. Carteret Historical Research Association, 1982.
White, Julia S. "History of North Carolina Yearly Meeting." *Bulletin of Friends' Historical Society of Philadelphia* 3, no. 1 (1909): 2–14.
Winslow, Randolph Rev. "*Winslow, Nathan*." NCPedia, https://www.ncpedia.org.
Wood, Gordon C. *Empire of Liberty: A History of the Early Republic, 1789–1815*. Oxford University Press, 2009.
Woolman, John. *The Journal of John Woolman*. Edited by John G. Whittier. Houghton Mifflin, 1909.

INDEX

C

D

K

L

M

N

O

P

Q

R

S

T

U

V

W

ABOUT THE AUTHOR

Tim Allen taught history, religion, and humanities at the community college and university level for thirty years. He earned a BA in Religious Studies from the University of South Carolina–Columbia, an MA in Religious Studies from the University of North Carolina–Chapel Hill, and the PhD in Theological Studies from the Graduate Theological Foundation, where he was a McQuarrie Fellow. He also earned graduate hours in Early American History from the University of North Carolina–Greensboro. In 2006, he attended the Oxford Roundtable to explore issues of religion and state. His publications include *North Carolina Quakers: Spring Friends Meeting*; *Snow Camp, North Carolina*; and, with Steve Miller, *Slave Escapes and the Underground Railroad in North Carolina*. He lives in Snow Camp, North Carolina, a Quaker community and station on the Underground Railroad. He also serves as a docent for the Graham Historical Museum.